Anni Sennov

The Crystal Human
and the Crystallization Process
Part I

About the spirit's journey into our
bodies and our everyday lives

good adventures publishing

The Crystal Human and the Crystallization Process Part I
© 2010-11, Anni Sennov and Good Adventures Publishing

Font setting: Palatino Linotype
Layout: Carsten Sennov - www.good-adventures.com
Cover design: Michael Bernth - www.monovoce.dk
Drawings: Agnes Männik - www.oledkohal.com
Illustrations: Anni Sennov - www.annisennov.eu

Original title in Danish: Krystalmennesket & Krystalliseringsprocessen
Translated into English by: Pernille Kienle of Absolute Translations &
Editing - www.absolutetranslations.dk

ISBN 978-87-92549-00-6

Acknowledgments

I would like to thank everyone who has contributed to this book with their personal Crystallization stories. It takes courage to share your own personal experiences with others and, in particular, with strangers whom you may never meet in real life.

If you would like to contact one or more of the Aura Mediators who work with AuraTransformation™, and who contributed with their stories to this book, you can find the contact information for some of them on the website below. Alternatively, please contact the Aura Mediator Instructor™ in your country.

www.auratransformation.eu

You will find my contact information at the end of the book.

I would also like to thank the Estonian Aura Mediator™, Agnes Männik, for her fun way of illustrating several of the chapters in the book. In my opinion, Agnes' drawings speak a clear language of their own.

Please note:

There are a multitude of different consciousness-expanding methods around the world that, each in their own way, aim at increasing the consciousness in the aura and/or the body.

In this book I have chosen to refer to AuraTransformation™ only, which is the consciousness-expanding method I am personally most familiar with as this method was developed by me.

It is therefore up to you, the reader, to become acquainted with other methods that inspire you.

This book refers to selected planet energies within our solar system. If this knowledge is beyond your normal conceptual field, please do not despair as this only happens a few times in the book!

In the cases contained in 'The Crystal Human and the Crystallization Process Part I' and 'The Crystal Human and the Crystallization Process Part II', several Aura Mediators™, instructors and clients mention their personal experience with various health products. These statements are based on each individual's personal experience. You will have to create your own experience and not rely too much on other people's personal experiences in connection with your personal Crystallization Process.

Neither the manufacturers, who are not aware of the publication of these two books and the effect their products may have in relation to a Body Crystallization, nor I or Good Adventures Publishing can be held responsible for the effect the mentioned products have in relation to your individual Crystallization Process.

Preface

The journey in taking the two books 'The Crystal Human and the Crystallization Process Part I' and 'The Crystal Human and the Crystallization Process Part II' from the original Danish version into English has been a lengthy, interesting and challenging one for all those involved in the process.sdfsdf

The Danish translator was given a remit of endeavouring to keep the style of writing as close to the original, and to Anni's own written style, as possible. While this was successfully achieved, the end result was not necessarily a document that would be experienced as either fluid or cohesive in the English language. Subsequent reviews of the two books have endeavoured to 'Englishify' them and make it a little easier on the eyes of native English (or American) speakersl.

The reader may still experience 'The Crystal Human and the Crystallization Process Part I' and 'The Crystal Human and the Crystallization Process Part II' as a little heavy and complicated to read in places and it has been an intentional decision to leave the books as such. For each of us involved in the translation and review of the books, we have experienced energy and magic at work, through the words that Anni has written. It was decided that retaining the integrity of this 'energy in action' was more valuable than arriving at an elegant piece of writing. Whilst Anni is known for her writing skill and fluency in Danish, this does not translate equally well into English. Her writing (and her speaking), is direct, to the point and information rich. The reader is therefore encouraged to stay with information being conveyed, rather than become involved in whether the wording or phrasing sounds 'right' or 'English'. When information is accessed from Source, the energy that works through words is often more important than the wording itself.

Working with the material provoked, induced, and stimulated crystallisation symptoms within each of us involved, and at times these were a little 'challenging'. Working towards our own individual crystallisation is however, very important, for the smooth integration of this energy into our collective experience on Mother Earth in the run up to, through 2012 and beyond. We hope and wish for you a wonderfully transforming experience reading the two books, and at the very least to finish them feeling as if you had certainly learned something new.

June McGuire
Management Consultant and Holistic Therapist

Content

INTRODUCTION

My purpose in writing the two books 'The Crystal Human and the Crystallization Process Part I' and 'The Crystal Human and the Crystallization Process Part II' is to outline and explain to my readers, in a tangible way, what it is like to live with and within the Crystal Energy of the New Time; that is to say with Spirit fully or partially integrated into your body and your everyday life. I will also provide some insight into how the Spirit makes its way into our bodies and about those measures that are appropriate to ensure a balanced fusion of body and spirit.

To live with the Spirit fully or partially integrated into your body is a state that everyone, who passes the transition from the Indigo Energy of the 4th dimension to the Crystal Energy of the 5th dimension, will experience at some point in their lives. 'The Crystal Human and the Crystallization Process Part I' and 'The Crystal Human and the Crystallization Process Part II' are therefore directed at anyone with an interest in the Crystal Energy. They are also directed at all aura-transformed adults as well as those who are considering an AuraTransformation™, because an AuraTransformation™ leads individuals from the Soul Energy through the Indigo Energy into the Crystal Energy where their Body Crystallization is activated when the time is right.

Many books describe Spiritual Energy as a pure state of being, of a non-physical nature, with which we as humans can connect, through for example meditation and healing. By connecting with this pure state of being, which many choose to call our Higher Selves, we obtain direct contact with our pure spiritual consciousness outside our bodies. This, however, requires us to be at Soul level with our consciousness, which aura-transformed individuals and the Indigo and Crystal Children of today are not. Instead, they are spiritual beings, which for Crystal Humans means that they have their own truth and divine spark, as well as their earthly life missions, deeply hidden within the cell structure of their bodies.

Up until the summer of 1996 when my aura was transformed with the help of a good friend of mine, and without either one of us knowing beforehand what this would entail, I was in touch with my Spiritual Energy almost daily, i.e. my Higher Self, through either healing, meditation or channelling.

From around 2005, however, those energy tools became unnecessary in my life, as I was able instead to just close my eyes or sit quietly by myself with my eyes wide open, without focusing on anything in particular, whenever I felt the need to recharge or gather my thoughts. It also became easier for me to find the solution to various questions in my life when I needed an immediate answer. Simply by focusing on an instant calm within my body, the answers I sought literally popped out of my system. And it still works like that for me.

The difference between 1996 and today is simply that my Spiritual Energy is now a fully integrated part of my body. My aura is very close to my body, which is why I no longer need to travel far outside my body into the outermost aura layers whenever I wish to connect with my Spiritual Energy. This saves a lot of time and effort and has given me so much energy in my everyday life - energy to do the things I want, rather than having to set aside a certain amount of time every day to quietly connect with my inner self for directions on which way to go in life and where to turn next.

If you have a busy life like I do with several children living at home, a wonderful husband and an interesting job, each with great opportunities for development, it is undeniably challenging to find sufficient time in the daily routine to nurture the Spirit as a separate part of your life and personality. It is therefore extremely liberating when your body, mind and Spirit speak the same language in every way, without having to solve any internal conflict before clearly stating your opinion to the outside world on a given topic.

Whether I use my gut feeling or my intuition, or whether I check the feeling in my big toe, I always get the same answer because the Crystal

Energy has worked itself into every part of my body and my aura and therefore into my entire system.

Nowadays for me meditation, healing and other forms of personal energy balancing work are still very enjoyable and relaxing ways to bring calm, clarity, balance and perspective, and I still enjoy this from time to time. However this only gives me a feeling of having slept for a few more hours at night and does not give my system any extraordinary kick at all. On the other hand, I get a kick at a physical level on a daily basis when I act out my ideas and succeed in doing things.

During many years of work - firstly with astrology, followed by healing and then AuraTransformation™ and clairvoyance - I have encountered many interesting, spiritually seeking individuals who, through various kinds of energy work, have worked intensively and exclusively with a focus on the spiritual aspects of life. In my eyes however, the price of this pure spiritual focus has often been that they were forced to move their consciousness focus away from the physical world, and consequently away from their physical bodies and daily lives. The majority of those people have therefore ended up in situations where they lack awareness of their everyday lives regarding their finances, work, home, family, friends, raising children and relationships, if they have indeed been able to maintain a relationship.

Having a thorough knowledge of your Higher Self, and therefore your own spiritual and consciousness potential, is always good and on par with knowing your body very well, i.e. knowing your body's strengths and weaknesses. But why even remove the body consciousness, which is the only physical tool we as humans possess to change external circumstances in our lives and our environment as a whole? After all, the body is a visible, physical manifestation of man's spiritual potential in this earthly universe, so why disallow our body's worth? The body represents our physical mobility, and the Earth is precisely where we are expected to live our current lives and where we are supposed to express ourselves in relation to each other.

Rather than applying either/or solutions in our lives, where we as humans both act as and perceive ourselves as pure spiritual beings or as earthly individuals, we must combine the two worlds by helping the Spirit enter into our bodies. This will allow the Spirit to gain a foothold in our physical reality which fully matches the fundamental structure of the Crystal Energy, and that is how the spiritual and more dense material part of us can meet as one sphere in our body to work together with each other - a condition that allows things to work for us at various levels simultaneously, not just the physical or the Spiritual level.

The fusion of the body and the Spirit can be activated in earnest if a person undergoes an AuraTransformation™. Through this, we change from being non-autonomous Soul consciousness beings to autonomous and auto-didactic Indigo and Crystal Individuals. As such, we may have one or more specific missions in respect to our earthly lives, which we are expected to act out, and in which we have the freedom or free will to choose the path(s) to that goal. This is in huge contrast to a life at Soul level where everybody has been subject to a general, common consciousness similar to that of many animals but where Soul Individuals, as opposed to animals, are here in order to learn something new and to become wiser and more intelligent in different areas. At Soul level the intention was indeed for humans to acquire knowledge consisting of insight, understanding and development and furthermore integrating foreign energies with a view to possibly cooperating with those energies.

At first an AuraTransformation™ ties our pure spiritual consciousness from the outermost aura to our bodies where the energy takes form as a combined balancing and protecting energy body. In this way, our Spiritual Energy becomes visible to others through our personal charisma. Through an AuraTransformation™ the foundation is laid for directing a large part of the pure spiritual consciousness from our auras into our physical bodies. This is called the Crystallization Process and can be a very time-consuming process.

There are countless different consciousness-expanding methods around the world, which, each in their own way, aim at increasing consciousness in the aura and the body, either simultaneously or separately. Among these methods are EMF Balancing Technique® (Electromagnetic Field Balancing), DNA Activation, Accelerating DNA Recoding Process, often combined with Multi-Dimensional Keys of Compassion, and more. Since I know little about these methods, however, I have chosen to exclusively refer to AuraTransformation™ in my two books, as that is the conscious-ness-expanding method that I am personally most familiar with. I leave it up to you, the reader, to learn more about the aforementioned methods, or similar methods, should you feel inspired to do so.

In all its simplicity, the Body Crystallization Process aims to combine our spiritual consciousness and spiritual power with our physical aspects and, once this has happened, it will be much easier for us to fulfill our life mission. As such, we become more mobile at the physical, spiritual, psychological and mental levels, and it becomes easier for us to adjust to our environment or seek alternatives if situations are not working for us.

You see, Crystal Humans of the New Time don't mind making crucial changes in either their everyday lives or their lives in general in order to gain ultimate balance. They always work hard to reach their goals while making every effort to avoid imbalance in their lives. On the other hand, they may take a very direct approach towards those who are not making an adequate contribution to finding a balanced solution to a given pro-blem. When this happens, Crystal Humans are able to completely exclude those individuals from their lives and thoughts, and this can just as easily happen within the framework of family, friends and work. When Crystal Humans are confronted with injustice, backstabbing and ignorance, etc. they have no problem facing up to the individual(s) behind the smear campaign, and they have no problem going public with their discontent, since they play with open cards all the way and have nothing to hide from the outside world.

Only by letting the Spirit enter into the core of the matter and the physical substance, can we as humans increase the frequency in the heaviest and densest earthly and human energy layers, where everything is about survival, physicalisation and materialism.

This is knowledge that all Crystal Humans possess deep down at cell level. This is also why they realize that, if they are to succeed with their life mission, they must work hard to get to the bottom and clean out all dense, obdurate, physical energies and obstacles – at first within their auras – and then within their bodies and their immediate environment.

During the AuraTransformation™, all emotional imbalances are transformed and thereby completely disappear from the aura. These imbalances will therefore not interfere when you let go of any old physical memories deep down at cell level in connection with your Body Crystallization.

The Spirit should not integrate physical matter so quickly, however, that there is a risk that your body will perish or physically break down and in its hurry, the cell structure loses its physical coding and is unable to hold itself together. If the cell structure loses its physical coding, there is indeed a risk of cell dysplasia, which, in extreme cases, can develop into for example cancer or immunodeficiency disorders. It is therefore vital to take extra care of our physical bodies while the Crystallization Process, and in particular the Crystallization of the body, takes place.

You see, neither our physical body nor our physical planet is able to adjust quickly to new and unfamiliar circumstances. Not even if we try to support the process by sending out lots of positive thoughts. It takes so much longer to carry out any development, whether spiritual or technological, at a physical level than it does at a Spiritual level. For example with technological development, it is nowadays common for people to disassociate mentally from something if development happens too fast. Unfortunately, many people also develop physical allergies to for example electro-magnetic frequencies from PCs and mobile phones, which now must be considered an integral part of modern society. Many people have an almost similar reaction in connection with spiritual development, although in that case, their 'allergies' are of a more mental nature.

For me personally, the Crystallization Phase of my body represented an extremely difficult time health-wise, as I became seriously ill with asthmatic eczema for the second time in my life. This went on for several months at the end of 2003, until I got so sick and my skin was so damaged, that I agreed to receive large amounts of cortisone treatment, with the slight hope of holding together my physical body. I was unaccustomed to consuming chemically produced medication and it really compromised my personal values and beliefs at the time. However, I quickly came to realize that in this particular instance, the medication was able to do something that I myself was not; because it was basically able to hold my body and my entire skin together, although it also triggered several side effects, such as a severe increase in my body weight.

The decision to take chemically produced medication was, therefore, a very costly affair for me physically, but it was only after treatment, that I was able to initiate the very radical integration of my Spiritual Energy all the way down to the cell level of my body.

My body, which of course is the dense and physical part of my energy, was simply unable to cope in the fight against my strong Spiritual Energy even though originally, the intention was for the two to work in equal cooperation. You see, the Spiritual Fire and the desire for truth were burning uncontrollably within my system, to such an extent that my body and my skin lost all its moisture. Back then I didn't understand the overall dilemma between the spiritual and the physical foundation at all in the way I understand it now. I didn't understand how fundamentally irreconcilable those two forces are, but my illness helped me to really gain clarity about the problem, so I ended up better able to accept the spirit's slow entry into the earthly physicality.

Fortunately, after a long battle, I regained my physical balance, and with the benefit of hindsight I actually find it fascinating that I became so wise regarding the very concept of Spiritual Energy through experiencing the gradual breakdown of my physical body right before my eyes. I would like to add, though, that it is now very difficult for me to recall all the physical pain that my physical breakdown entailed at the time. All I know for sure is that I have absolutely no desire to repeat the experience.

My conclusion to this course of events turned out to be the following: If I, as a spiritually conscious individual, was incapable of containing the pure Spiritual Energy within my physical body, then how could other less spiritually conscious people contain the influx of Spiritual Energy into their physical bodies?

Suddenly I understood that if Spirit in its purest form were suddenly to occupy Earth, as is the true wish of many spiritual people, the physical structure of the planet would simply collapse. All human development as well as development of all kinds of physical intelligence, knowledge and insight would therefore be completely wasted; when the Spirit burns through everything, only the essence of everything remains, which corresponds to a pure state of being, but with no physical memory on which to build human development. If this were to happen, Earth would have to start all over by developing human consciousness from scratch. Better to move ahead a bit more slowly but surely, taking both Spirit and matter into consideration at the same time and in a balanced way.

Although you are free to choose the speed of the Body Crystallization yourself, I do not recommend opening up completely to the integration of the pure spiritual consciousness in your body. I recommend that my clients, and now you as well, take one step at a time in your Crystallization Process instead and do things at a speed that you can handle. Don't look at what others do, as we all have our own individual way of integrating our spiritual consciousness into our bodies, which you will hopefully appreciate when you have read the many different Crystallization cases that I have included in 'The Crystal Human and the Crystallization Process Part I' and 'The Crystal Human and the Crystallization Process Part II'.

My sincere hope is that the two books will help you gain a better insight into your personal Crystallization Process, no matter where you are in the process, so that you may feel inspired to do things that are *right just for you.*

Kind regards,

Anni Sennov
Copenhagen, Denmark, April 2009

„NEW CONSCIOUSNESS RISING"

THE NEW TIME ENERGY

The New Time Energy
has become the energy of our time

New energies and consciousness impulses are constantly arriving on Earth. Therefore it is actually somewhat misleading to use the term the New Time Energy in connection with the Indigo and Crystal Energies, as these two forms of energy represent the energy of our time, with which we surround ourselves in the years around 2000.

In the future, we will continue to experience new eras in the history of Earth, each revolutionary in its own way, for the dissemination of new consciousness trends and technologies, which usually go hand in hand. So why is it that the exact time around the year 2000 by many spiritual people has been defined as much more innovative and more New Time-like than other eras? Among other places, the answer to this can be found within astrology where it is explained that around the end of the second millennium, our solar system has shifted its consciousness from the Age of Pisces into the Age of Aquarius, although this has yet to happen at a physical level. The shift described, which according to research is really based on a visual illusion from the Earth's perspective, will prompt big, long-term global change for humanity as a whole as well as for our values. This will mean a number of things for the people of Earth, most importantly perhaps that individual sacrifice will no longer be required for the common good, as was the case with Jesus in the early Age of Pisces around year 30 A.D.

At the same time, humankind will also by-and-large change from being power-seeking and materialistic to focusing on human values and collaboration across religion, race and other differences instead.

> As for consciousness, the turn of the second millennium repre-
> sents a significant transition in the Earth's form of government
> with regard to consciousness – from Soul consciousness to
> spiritual consciousness. Specifically, this means that all new-
> born Indigo Children are born with a pure Spiritual Energy
> in their auras and all newborn Crystal Children are born with
> a pure Spiritual Energy in their auras as well as their bodies.

Indigo and Crystal Children are thus not born with a Soul aura that matches that of their parents' and grandparents' energy structure which, until
now, was part of a bigger hierarchical reincarnation and development
plan for the Earth. Indigo and Crystal Children are all born outside the
Soul plan which is finally to be phased out during the time up until the
year 2050, if not earlier.

What this means is that all future Crystal Children and all adult Crystal
Humans who, through an AuraTransformation™ have had their aura
transformed into a Crystal aura and who at a later point have undergone
a Body Crystallization or vice versa (in which case they were first body
crystallized and then underwent an AuraTransformation™), are therefore
whole individuals who act as pure energy sources carrying the optimum
divine potential.

In this connection, the Indigo Energy represents the initial stage of the Crystal Energy where all individuals are still connected to the Earth's overall
joint consciousness, but where they possess a much more powerful and
intuitive energy than the Soul Energy is able to access. Indigo Humans
are able to channel cosmic divine energy, new thoughts and ideas as well
as healing to themselves and others from the joint consciousness, without
always being able to see the full energy picture themselves. Indigo Humans
therefore still act as channels for all higher vibrational energy, as do Soul
Humans, until one day they crystallize in their auras and their bodies as
a result of their own consciousness development, when their Spiritual

Energy becomes fully integrated into their bodies.

With the Crystal Energy fully integrated, we as humans will be able to act as pure sources for our own inherent impulses concerning our divinity and life in general. It is our job to live it out at a physical level here on Earth, in different ways, and in accordance with our respective life missions.

Not until we are completely crystallized in our aura and body will the energy in the aura fully close around us according to a specific, harmonized constellation of energies consisting of the following elements: Fire, Water, Earth and Air. Through this, we will become pure individual divine sources made up of a self-rechargeable, closed circuit that is completely capable of quickly recharging itself given the right conditions.

Parents and adults as responsible role models

When we humans try to describe the concept of consciousness, words are simply not adequate as a means of expression. This is a fact that most spiritual people are sure to agree with 100%. It is therefore incredibly important to always have your 'inner bridge builder' activated when the topic of conversation is on personal and spiritual consciousness, in order that the true essence of other peoples' messages is better understood.

It is for this reason that many spiritual people choose to activate their 'inner bridge builder' early on in life, and it is this that enables an added openness and understanding with other spiritual people, who are just as open and outspoken in relation to the outside world as they are to themselves.

Regardless of nationality, consciousness, cultural and social background, this openness allows people to understand each other's way of thinking at a higher and subtler level, and therefore facilitates arriving at a mutual understanding. People are then able to disregard the linguistic wording in these consciousness contexts, which is a great advantage when people meet across industries and borders, where different cultures are often an obstacle. If we were unable to communicate across external physical differences, the doors of Heaven and of the Spirit would quickly close between us human beings here on Earth. This would only leave a foundation for physical, emotional and mental inter-human relations, with no room for spirituality, creativity, vision, flexibility and a willingness to change.

A willingness to change is particularly important in the New Time - our time - so that people are able to find a new platform in life that matches the Earth's ongoing consciousness upgrade. If we as humans cannot keep up with the planet's general development and the development of society, particularly those of us who are adults, then there will be no one to guide all those confident Indigo Children and spiritually intelligent Crystal Children who, around the turn of the second millennium found, and will continue to find, their way to Earth. You see many of these new children don't have experience of life on Earth from previous incarnations, although the majority of their parents do, who were born into the Soul Energy.

Children and adolescents of today all need guidance in living a balanced physical life, and this guidance ought to come from their parents as well as many of the adults that they come into contact with in their daily lives.

Nowadays it is much more imperative that adults take responsibility for teaching children how to manage and control their heightened consciousness, so that this might be transformed into constructive behaviour and positive action on a physical level.

The alternative is that we run the risk of children and adolescents taking over homes and society in general without having learned how to manage self-control, and where parents and other adults choose to give in to young people's wants and pace, etc. 'for the sake of peace', completely incapable of keeping up themselves.

This takeover is bound to happen, whether or not parents and other adults set clear, everyday boundaries for children and adolescents. It will happen, even if children and adolescents do not have the academic and human expertise or the life experience, on which to base their high-frequency and often far too fast lifestyle. Basically, the takeover will occur because many of today's adults choose not to act as responsible role models for their children, e.g. by getting directly and actively involved in the development of society. Any such development naturally will be the foundation for any further development on which our children will establish their personal values and commitments once they are adults and have children of their own.

If parents are actively engaged with other people, in various projects or society in general, this usually has a great impact on their children with the result that they themselves will also similarly become engaged. If parents are not engaged, children will not learn at home how they themselves connect with the world, or in their relationships with others. If this is the case, they may have to learn this from other adults in their everyday lives, which may be asking a lot of people who are not within the family circle.

Once the high-frequency, creative energy of the New Time really kicks in with the young people of this generation, this will trigger the launch of many 'air balloons' in record time carrying visionary projects towards unknown destinations. The success of these projects is not guaranteed and some may run aground due to a lack of knowledge of the route, weather conditions, fuel consumption, etc., while others are sure to reach their destination, based on parent encouragement as well as the young people's skills and pre-planning.

Sadly, in these consciousness-expanding transitional periods, reality much too often has a language of its own which, in order to miss this one has to be physically deaf or blind as well as spiritually reserved.

Unfortunately, central to most problems involving children and adolescents when teachers in general and parents in particular do not take it upon themselves to guide young people in a way that is relevant to their lives and daily reality of young people the young will simply find a way to live out their lives away from the eyes of their parents and other adults. There is nothing new in this. The significant difference is that today's adolescents are energetically much more powerful than their predecessors and when things go wrong, it will normally be on a bigger and much more extensive scale.

Today, responsible adult guidance is more important than ever before.

Children used to have an energy capacity equivalent to a normal bomb. Today, their energy capacity has reached atomic potential. While the development potential and resources

available is breathtaking, it is also potentially fatal if used incorrectly or unwisely.

Assuming that most parents possess some knowledge about social capabilities and society, local culture etc, and since children are arriving in this world with completely new and radical thoughts that allow room for both the individual and the collective at the same time, there may indeed be a good foundation for an interesting and positive development of life on Earth. Alternatively there is the potential for a mass revolt by young people!

Due to a general lack of openness and willingness to change on the part of adults and the older generation, most parents will continue to be at least one generation behind with the integration, understanding and living out of the new energies. When it comes to consciousness, all children and young people will generally have a permanent head start on their physically adult advisors, which is what their parents and teachers are expected to be. This situation firmly puts the children and adolescents in the driver's seat and the parents and the teachers, etc. in the back seat. Therefore, my best advice to all parents and adults who socialize with children and adolescents on a daily basis is to change the positions by becoming more conscious themselves and active in their role model, if they haven't already done so.

Fortunately there are quite a few high-frequency adults who have no problem keeping up with the energy of these children and adolescents, and who feel deeply inspired by their alertness, resourcefulness, sense of invention and great energy at home, at school and within their sports organizations etc. However, most adults find it hard to keep up with the high level of daily, physical pace unless they are extremely fit themselves, and the young also often find it difficult to keep up themselves. While it has always been important for parents and adults to provide children and young people with positive guidance and clear boundaries, it is all the more imperative now.

Children who are familiar with rules, respect and cooperation from home and who know how to handle these qualities in their lives, will find it undeniably easier to associate and cooperate with adults other than their own parents, e.g. at school or in connection with extra-curricular activities. In addition, children and adolescents should be able to move around freely outside and in the streets, without the company of adults, and without being a nuisance to their environment, once they have reached the appropriate age.

It is such a joy for everybody when children and adolescents are able to conduct themselves in a balanced way within the framework of our current society. If we must have a revolt because the framework for children is too tight, too limited or wrong, then let it be the parents who fight for their children's cause. Children themselves should not have to rebel in order to be heard.

It is important that parents listen to their children's opinions, so that they are able to manage and address any imbalances in their children's lives until they have grown old enough to speak up for themselves. Once these young adults are able to speak up for themselves they will do so in a balanced way, based on the guidance they have received at home.

Due to their limited life experience, children do not yet possess many ways of expressing themselves, which is why all kinds of revolt are often expressed in an extremely simplified way consisting of anger, despair, pessimism and/or physically violent behaviour. If these actions occur much too frequently, resulting in often rebellious behaviour, naturally this places children and adolescents in a poor light within their environment.

It requires extremely transgressive measures for children and adolescents to become very closed up or aggressive every single day, which is why general rebellious behaviour can usually be nipped in the bud if the parents and other adults in the lives of the children and the adolescents are aware of this in time. Therefore, parents and other adults must be alert regarding the(ir) children's behaviour and daily activities and act in time, as it is the parents' responsibility to raise their children properly.

There will always be children and adolescents, who are completely maladjusted to such an extent that they need external professional help in order to be able to function here on Earth. In those cases, both parents and teachers often have to realize that they are up against uncontrollable consciousness powers in the child and the adolescent, which neither they, nor the prevailing child care and school systems of our society can handle. In those cases, parents should not start thinking of normal or alternative ways of raising their children, but rather seek advice from professionals within this area.

New impulses and energies are always interesting, whether they come from children or adults, but they are not always particularly welcome, especially if they arrive out of the blue and attempt to undermine everything that already exists.
These days many children and adolescents use the highly effective Indigo method of persuasive power to sign up parents, teachers and others to their way of doing things, or their latest new idea. The idea may be good, but the timing may not be right to realize it. This is when adults need to be especially mature and firm and resist the persuasive strength of the Indigos.

During the Crystal Energy era the concept of timing becomes even more decisive as to, whether or not we as humans achieve positive results in connection with the realization of our good ideas. It is extremely important for us to have a good gut feeling and a good inner feeling when launching new thoughts and projects; otherwise we may not achieve the best possible results. Crystal Humans, however, are masters of the concept of timing, unlike Soul and Indigo Humans. You see, Crystal Humans always know, whether or not things will work. They also know when the time is right to launch a certain project and it is totally impossible to persuade them to get involved in half-projects. On the other hand, they are capable of getting 100% involved in a split second, if the project and the timing feel right, and they always succeed with their projects.

Concepts, such as timing, integration, understanding, openness, respect, willingness to change and innovation are all extremely important elements in connection with the New Time Energy's entry here on Earth. In the years leading up to 2012, when the Crystal Energy will have its real breakthrough in our society here on Earth, parents will become increasingly aware of these qualities. This will either be because their children will need to learn the meaning of the above-mentioned qualities, or because the children possess those qualities from birth and must teach them to their parents.

In this new world, you may wonder from time to time who is the parent and who is the child in a parent-child relationship, as the Crystal Children are born as completely crystallized individuals with a Crystal clear consciousness and a focus on living out these values and qualities. These are all aspects of the New Time Karma.

The New Time Karma

Within the Crystal Energy, which will continue to be integrated more and more in our society during the years up to 2012 and then be fully lived out in the years to follow, the concept of karma no longer has two facets that make up the essence of the concept *'reap what you have sown'*.

Because the world has grown and is now much bigger and much more varied since the origin of karma, each individual is now expected to both relate and adjust to a reality that is much more varied and that holds many more aspects than our predecessors had to deal with.
The importance of firstly creating and then maintaining a general balance within your personal life and also your consciousness is thereby greatly intensified.

The essence of the karma concept will always be to reap what you have sown, but with the Crystal Energy this concept has been significantly upgraded and updated.

In the years around the turn of the second millennium, the karma concept has had several essential qualities added, with a focus on each individual contributing positively towards the collective and the surrounding community. At the same time, they must remember to focus on their own personal development and balance, since the wholeness, which, depending on the actual situation, could be the society, the environment, your family, friends, colleagues, Mother Earth etc. including yourself as a part of the wholeness, and the individual must be in balance at all times.

Please note that when I use the term 'wholeness' throughout the book, I am referring to things as a whole. 'Wholeness' means 'the whole' which originates from (w)holiness with its many different aspects of life, and allows room for everything, including our differences. The term 'wholeness' leaves plenty of space for all people so they are free to do whatever they want, and to do so in their own way – hopefully to the benefit of the 'wholeness'.

I believe that 'wholeness' is a Scandinavian phenomenon, as I often hear the word 'oneness' used in English-speaking countries. To me, 'wholeness' best describes what I refer to in this book. I sincerely hope you understand my way of expressing things.

In the Crystal Energy, the karma concept includes concepts such as social and personal responsibility, respect, balance, justice, boundary setting, consequence, and gathering and disseminating information, which is why the meaning of karma as an isolated concept with two facets and a simple symbolism is in many ways changing to be a thing of the past in the minds of modern-day people.

The New Time Karma is all about the following:

- What you signal to others and to the world in general, will be returned to you in the form of real-time karma.

  With the Indigo and Crystal Energies, your actions will have consequences much more quickly than at Soul level, where many people still live according to a predetermined life plan and will continue to for a number of years into the future. Therefore, you must think carefully before you act out your short-term as well as your long-term decisions and plans in life. The settlement of Karma, however, does not always happen the same day, even though it happens much faster than it used to, and it does not always involve those individuals, scenarios and places, etc. that were involved originally.

- Viewing yourself as part of a bigger whole which, over the coming years, will be involving New Time-oriented individuals as well as individuals with Soul consciousness.

- Being respectful of yourself and others, no matter what their standpoint may be regarding their understanding of consciousness. Respect of personal property, personal integrity and decision-making etc. will be significant so long as the intention of others' actions and their personal conduct is well meaning.

- When making your personal plans, it is important to take into consideration both your own needs and the needs of others and ensure that you have a balance between your personal relationships and your goals, in your daily life and in general.

- It is important to be fair. The rules, regulations, rights and agreements etc. that apply to you, equally apply to others, whether in your relationships with your partner, your family, at work, etc.

- You should be aware of your own boundaries and those of others, whether they are your co-players or your opponents. By being familiar with social and cultural norms, both at home and abroad wherever you travel through work, on holidays or in your spare time, you will always get on better with people.

- Maintaining your own personal boundaries is important, in relation to both yourself and others. For instance, it is of no use if others respect, accept and follow the personal rules and boundaries you have set for your home, your relationship with your partner or at work, etc., if you do not respect and follow your own rules and boundaries yourself.

- It is important to become the best you can be in any way you can. This will benefit not only you, but also the wholeness that you are part of, whether this be your family, your relationship, your community, your country, your organization of interest, your ideology, etc.

- In the New Time, knowledge brings with it responsibility, so the more you know, the more you are obliged to teach for the benefit of others - because what else should you use your knowledge for?

- The more knowledge you acquire in a variety of fields, the wider your perspective and the greater will be your capacity to focus, as you are able to separate the essential from the non-essential. You will then also become better able to share your knowledge with others, so that they can be helped in moving on in their respective lives and personal and/or social development.

The Earth
- a planet with conflicts of interests

Many highly evolved people have asked themselves the following questions countless times:

"Why is the expansion of consciousness taking so long?"

and

"Why doesn't the divine power just hurry up and turn up the highest possible frequencies on Earth, so that we may quickly increase the earthly consciousness to the benefit of all?"

The answers to these questions are actually quite simple. You see, the frequencies have already been increased as much as possible and at the fastest possible speed, without the physical planet and various social structures around the world exploding before our eyes. This is because Earth is made up of various forms of energy, magnetism, frequencies and consciousness, etc., which in their respective foundations each originate from the surrounding planets in our solar system as well as planets in far-away galaxies. The Earth therefore acts as a planet for joint development and a platform for our solar system and does not have the status of an independent planet with the right to make its very own decisions.

The divine intention is, however, for the Earth to act as an independent planet at some point in the future, but this will not happen until - through our actions - mankind can show that it consists of a united people despite internal differences.

Every single time a big decision has to be made, which pertains to the future development of the Earth, there are many different consciousness authorities present at the table, similar to the UN (the United Nations). These originate from respective planets within the solar system and, similarly to the UN and the EU (the European Union) and other general earthly authorities, they must agree on common general future goals for the Earth, which, unfortunately, is not always possible. This is why sometimes, although a general agreement has been reached through a majority vote, the parties who disagree try to work against the majority behind the scenes.

This also parallels the current situation on Earth itself, where there is an endless number of authorities at different consciousness levels who also need to come to an agreement, each with different interests in 'Project Earth', and therefore wish to have a say in the development of any agreements.

Everything on this planet – even the smallest of structures – exists in a similar way, at one or more consciousness levels, through one (or many) of the planets that inhabit our solar system.

All inhabitants of the Earth get their spiritual, mental, emotional, social and technological inspiration, both positive and negative, from those planets where their energy originates. It is therefore not equally beautiful everywhere in Heaven and in Hell, in accordance with the energies of the various planets in the solar system as well as certain other places out there in the big Universe. This is reflected in the limited, selfish and anti-social behaviour of many people.

When energies from various planets are mixed, as is happening in these times of integration, the result is not always known beforehand. Generally speaking the idea is, however, that the result of collaboration across borders, cultures and beliefs, will eventually result in a more holistic view of people, life and the world.

Since the Earth, in its physical fundamental structure, is an extremely material and dense planet, and since the ultimate goal of physical earthly intelligence is reproduction, propagation and physical creation, our planet has, right from the beginning, been a target for testing of spiritual power in relation to material physicality; and all with the intention of, one day, returning the Universe and the physicality back to the Spirit and the nothingness.

Meanwhile, Project Earth has turned out to be much harder to handle from a spiritual point of view than previously anticipated, even though there has been much spiritual focus on guiding cosmic intelligence and insight to Earth throughout time, which, up until now, has only happened in small discrete doses.

The objective of supplying cosmic intelligence is to increase the spiritual frequencies, so that various, negative physicality can no longer continue to form without a general, positive objective. Today we are seeing cynicism, violence and destruction, etc. used much too often, with the objective of enabling people all over to reach their own personal goals and those of their countries, without consideration of the needs of other peoples or nations.

The Earth therefore does not house a clear, unilateral energy that can quickly be transformed into a more spiritual focus, simply because people possess a large spiritual capacity and the best of intentions. It is not easy to merge all the different contemporary energies, which to date has caused the Earth to be divided into continents and countries and then areas and cities, respectively, just as it is not easy to merge two individuals into one physical being.

At a Spiritual level you can easily merge several consciousnesses into one consciousness and make them co-operate productively at different consciousness levels, including the physical level. At the physical level, however, history has taught us all that human isolation and physical separation between people who love each other seems much more natural and honourable for most inhabitants of the Earth, than merging emotionally and mentally with another human being in an effort to attain a unique dualism regarding consciousness and humanity. In this context, cultivating the lost love and the lonely lives of great artists, in connection with the creation of their masterpieces, speaks a clear language of its own.

Right from the beginning, the Earth was inhabited by many, large civilizations with very different consciousness backgrounds and approaches. Societies that have all attempted to build up a unique society of their own based on their respective convictions that were expected to last for a long time into the future. None of those societies, however, have managed to stay spiritually and physically balanced to such an extent that they were able to survive for thousands of years in the physicality of our world society. The reason for this is that if we as a society and as individuals do not ensure a progressive development at a physical level that corresponds to our spiritual development, all progress will literally fall flat.

There is no value in building up a beautiful aura and a divine energy towards people and projects where the energy reaches far into the sky, if neither the people nor the projects have a solid foundation in the physical reality. In this way a non-physical reality is created where everything happens at a mental and emotional level and where the spiritual reality cannot be realized and conveyed to the outside world at a physical level.

And not only are our ideas and projects not realized, you also run the risk of being overcome, without warning, by physical and mental illness, as there is no balance between ideas and reality within your system, and also because you may not be taking care of your physical body as well as it needs you to do.

In other words, it is necessary to have balance between Spirit and matter, i.e. between your consciousness and your physical body. So when spiritual people, whom we must assume are more conscious about their physical life missions than physically oriented people, are unable to balance Spirit and matter in their lives, how would more physically oriented people react if the energy's rotation speed here on Earth were dramatically increased at short notice?

You can almost see the insanity spread as only a few people would be capable of keeping themselves together physically and mentally. It is also hard to imagine how extremely spiritually oriented individuals, who have chosen to live a secluded life away from the stress and noise of the physical world, only in touch with themselves and their equals, would be physically able to help provide food, money and other daily necessities for people in need, in order to be able to function.

Instead, many spiritual people choose to stay at home by themselves or in a forum with equal-minded spiritual people and help by sending light to needy people of the world, only to then sanctify their own efforts. But there are still only very few people on this Earth who can get physically full from spiritual light. The worst-case scenario is that they become even more physically depleted than they are already, as pure Spiritual Energy totally undermines the physical structure of the human body. I can personally testify to this after experiencing the overwhelming entry of the Spirit and the light into my physical body at the beginning of my Body Crystallization. You see, in many ways the spirit's entry into the body is similar to the entry of physical death, only in small doses at a time, to which many cancer patients can testify. So, the concept of light in its purest and most high frequency form is definitely no joke. It is not something you should spread wildly as if it were some divine gift to all of humanity, as quite often, it breaks down more than it builds up.

Light on the other hand, is great for breaking down extremely dense physicality and matter, so it is for a good reason that the words enlightenment (*oplysning*) and dissolution (*opløsning*) are very closely related in the Scandinavian languages.

You can use light for enlightening and dissolving physical imbalances, but you cannot build up physicality through light, as light undermines and dissolves all physical density. Poor people in Africa and elsewhere in the world thus need practical solutions in order for their physical bodies to survive and act as a home to their Spiritual Energy. They do not need light for enlightening and dissolution of their already weakened physical bodies and physical environment.

You cannot use light to pay the bills either, which many spiritual people have realized already, which is why it is far more humane and respectful to donate money to physically distressed people and thus enable them to buy their own food and pay their own rent, etc.

As illustrated, it is a huge mistake to assume that the world's poor are fighting to integrate Spiritual Energy. Instead, they are fighting to survive at a physical level and this cannot be rectified through spirituality. Who knows, maybe those people arrived here with too much Spiritual Energy and are here to learn about the value of the physicality by experiencing its severe deprivation here on Earth?

It may seem completely unrealistic by today's standards to merge the two polar opposites – i.e. the spiritually and physically survival-oriented people – into one homogeneous unity where everybody can enjoy each other, but nonetheless it is one of the overall future goals of the Earth.

To begin with, however, the main general consciousness focus is not to make parents around the world freak out at an inner level about having to take onboard the new, extremely high consciousness frequencies that the divinity has decided to equip their children with.

The divine source (God) uses the children to increase the influx of spiritual consciousness to the Earth on an ongoing basis. In addition, physical illness plays a deciding role in lifting the energy frequencies of people's bodies as well as

> making them conscious of their own priorities, values and lifestyles. In particular, we experience this when various unspecified flu-like epidemics rage in our countries.

Currently only a few people on this Earth have the New Time's high-frequency balanced Crystal Energies integrated into their auras and bodies to such an extent that they can avoid reacting to an influenza virus and life-threatening bacteria, etc. - viruses and bacteria that, at a Spiritual level, represent very cleansing and frequency-enhancing conditions for the energy of the physical body, although it is not experienced as such at a physical level at all.

During a time of serious illness, the physical body is pushed to its limits regarding strength and vitality, while the Spiritual Energy completely has the upper hand until the body, after fighting hard, is able to re-establish the physical-spiritual balance at a new and often higher consciousness level. This is why many people feel as if they were returning from the land of the dead after having been totally worn out by illness, once they return to their normal lives. So, Spiritual Energy in its pure form is definitely no laughing matter, once it makes its way into the body and takes the upper hand.

To counteract the spirit's entry into the body, it is important, at a physical level, to be aware that different viruses and bacteria can also be due to lack of hygiene as well as the effect from pesticides and processed and genetically modified products, etc. These are products, which, in different ways, represent physical structures that the physical body is not predisposed to relate to and is therefore unable to handle.

The body does not instinctively know how to break down these unknown structures into transformable particles which are to its benefit - if it is at all possible for the body to take any advantage of pesticides and such. The body therefore activates the entire immune system, including allergic reactions, fever and flu-like symptoms, etc. This is why it is extremely important to be vigilant about what we eat, drink, the detergent we use, as well as our clothes and materials for our homes, at our jobs and other places. We must also protect the personal balance between our bodies and our spirits, so that neither gets the upper hand.

Allowing the pure Spiritual Energy to enter Earth all at once is therefore not recommended, as all existing physical material would then be destroyed and lost there and then. Alternatively, the Earth would become sick and crippled. It is also no use allowing relatively large amounts of Spiritual Energy into unconscious human bodies over a short space of time, as those individuals would then react as if they were going through menopause or behave as if it were summer and extremely hot outside.

This may sound completely unrealistic, but all of a sudden everybody would have to be extra careful when associating with others, in traffic as well as in society in general, as many people simply would not be able to gather their thoughts in the 'heat' and with the high energy frequencies. Not even if it were winter or autumn outside. Something simply snaps in the brain, and similarly with regard to one's perspective and temper, because it appears to be difficult to focus and stay calm and collected when lifted into the highest and cleanest spiritual frequencies that lie within the Fire element - hence the heat-generating energy.

Creating a unique world society is therefore an extremely long process with many stakeholders, who all wish to have part of their unique energy represented in the new common earthly unity and consciousness.

The overall objective is therefore to get as many people as possible to join in the Earth's next development phase – the Crystallization Phase – which will seriously begin at society level in 2012. At that point in time Venus, which in our solar system represents the Crystal Energy's spiritual base, will really enter the picture with its impact on consciousness. Each individual initiative that is taken during the years up until

then with a view to prepare for Aura and Body Crystalliza-
tions and to create clarity out and about in society, is merely to
prepare for the big Crystallization kick-off all over the planet.

Crystal Energy vs. Golden Energy

Many spiritual people have already started to develop an interest in integrating the Golden Energy, which represents the consciousness dimension after the Crystal Energy. However, they are all a bit too early because, in reality, not many people know what the Golden Energy consists of, other than the fact that it is perceived to be metallic, as it contains all mineral and metallic molecules. Only few people know why we must first integrate the Crystal Energy to optimize the benefit from the Golden Energy's presence in our physical and spiritual lives.

The Golden Energy matches that of the Crystal Energy in every way, only it expresses itself more fluently and freely, yet firmly.

The fluent and yet firm Golden Energy structure, however, cannot be fully integrated, until we as humans are fully crystallized in our auras and bodies, so that our spirits and bodies are capable of expressing themselves with one physical energy expression, i.e. our personal expression. The fact that many spiritual people have a more subtle energy expression of the Golden Energy resting within their aura is because they carry a spiritual picture with them into their physical lives. There are just as many people around this Earth, though, who have a physical impression of the Golden Energy hidden deeply inside their cell consciousness.

It is up to the majority of spiritual and very earthly-oriented people to manifest and materialize these energy images at a physical level here on Earth at some point in the future, as part of their personal Dharma/life missions. The Golden Energy thus lies ready in many people's spiritual and physical consciousness with a view to being realized at a later point. The realization, however, will not occur until they have fully integrated the Crystal Energy into their auras and bodies as well as their personal network, which together are the foundation for the combined and balanced, responsible and structured Venus-Earth platform, which the Golden Energy will build on at a later point.

The Golden Energy's firm, and at the same time flexible, physical form originates from the flowing, subtle, spiritual intelligence and insight, that many spiritual people bring along in their auras when they are born. This energy is very visible to the environment, when the aura is combined with the dense, physical energy that makes up the human body and the Earth.

In the years from 2012, when the first Golden Crystallized People start to enter society with their new ideas and initiatives, they will already know how to follow the social flow elegantly, while they are able to weave all their innovation into the earthly energy flow without discord.

Many present-day people have, in their spiritual and physical consciousness, a strong memory of recreating something big that once was. However, there is no use trying to recreate old realities that could not survive in the long run. It is a fact that none of the great, early civilizations have managed to survive to this day, in the shape and form it held at that time, although many people who were once there still glorify those societies.

Instead we need to create 'a New Earth' using expert knowledge of the past, the present and the future, by building this future energy structure from the ground up. And this time around, the foundation must be solid and flexible, with an innate balance of Spirit and matter. The idea is for the physical and spiritual intelligences to work together - two very opposite powers that each represent very different ways of relating to life and human consciousness – and for these to not fight and work against each other, such as on Atlantis, which unfortunately came to an end.

All spiritual people must therefore learn to function in a basic earthly life by passing through the earthly matrix so that they understand the physical forces they are up against, when they are working to realize their earthly life missions and their individual Dharma at a later point. The most important thing in connection with assuming their physical bodies and the build-up of their 'new earthly connection', is to integrate a variety of codes into their consciousness that are relevant for them, so that they can pass through all earthly obstacles, regardless of the nature of these obstacles, and end up as whole human beings on the other side.

Once these codes are fully integrated and the Crystallization has been completed, all spiritual people will be able to find the exact same answers in the basic earthly matrix in the future, which they previously were only able to obtain in the spiritual world through the outermost part of their aura.

Many earthly and extremely physically oriented people often choose a completely different direction than that of spiritual people, when they wish to integrate the Spirit into their everyday lives. This is because they know the earthly matter inside out from birth, and often also from previous lives in the earthly consciousness sphere.

They usually become acquainted with the Spirit in its pure form through the illness or death of people close to them, as well as through divorce, lay-offs, accidents, etc., which for a while makes them lose control of their physical lives. Nothing can make people dig deeper and faster into their physical body consciousness in search of a more profound meaning of life, than physically violent events. Their individual life missions are thereby exposed, giving them something new to be dedicated to, which is also why they often change the direction of their lives.

No spiritually or earthly oriented individuals wish to leave this life without having realized themselves first. It simply seems unnatural to not realize yourself in the earthly universe. The main difference in each respective fundamental outlook on life is simply that spiritual people know that they are here for a reason. Earthly oriented people often believe that this

is the only life they will ever have, and therefore wish to manifest themselves as much as possible during their physical lifetime. They therefore
wish to make a tangible difference by leaving a physical mark that will
remain when they leave this Earth, as their lives would have otherwise
been meaningless.

In brief, those people wishing to contribute in their own way to manifesting and materializing some physical creations, conditions and energies, etc. that will endure in the history of the Earth, have intentions that
are fundamentally identical to their spiritual counterparts but with their
consciousness focused on something very different.

At some point within the foreseeable future, the flexible, visionary, Golden
Energy therefore really needs to be present, in order to weave together
various human initiatives across borders, cultural differences, etc. There
will be a great need for resourceful people to create far-reaching and
flexible solutions for the world in a simple, balanced and elegant way;
solutions that the majority of people on Earth are able to accept and follow, no matter what their consciousness is like.

Let us forget about recreating great societies of the past, e.g. Atlantis and
Lemuria that were unable to create a unique consciousness level here on
Earth by combining and balancing the great differences between light and
darkness, Spirit and matter, responsibility and pleasure in mankind. The
main task of the qualities of Crystal Energy during the period before and
after 2012, will be to balance very different perspectives around the Earth.

To begin with, however, these differences must be observed and clarified
and then all involved parties must be conferred with in order to identify
productive, usable solutions. Finally, the solutions must be realized and
manifested where needed. Not until then can flexibility occur in the earthly
sphere since the presence of the Golden Energy represents a unique, intelligent and balanced consciousness level in a physical form.

It should be pointed out, though, that in this context, the Golden Time represents yet another consciousness phase in the forward development of the Earth. This is why, from a spiritual perspective, there is no need to idealize it until we have experienced how the exact energy can influence our crystallized bodies as well as our auras on a daily basis.

In no way does the Golden Time represent the end of the Earth's development. On the contrary, it is the beginning of even more developments that will find their way to Earth during the time after the entry of the Crystal Energy, based on the Crystal Energy's breakthroughs and experiences.

But, one thing at a time. First priority is the integration of the Crystal Energy; so that we as human beings may be able to assess which energies we are dealing with specifically, before we start looking at the Crystal Energy on a global scale. Alternatively, we run the risk of not being able to use the Golden Energy productively at all, which certainly contradicts the underlying plan for the Earth's current and future consciousness development.

THE CRYSTAL ENERGY

People's differences

There are just as many types of people as there are animals on this planet. The way, in which we view our planet and the great Universe, as well as the micro world in our immediate environment, is therefore very different. The reason for this is that we as humans have different consciousness levels and capacities in relation to external as well as internal influences and circumstances.

There are people, who are as big as gods in their personal consciousness and there are people, who are big and small inside in various forms, colours, varieties, etc. There are people, who think and act like elephants and predators, like rats and vermin, like squirrels and deer, so human variety is indeed plentiful.

Some people fight for peace, while others fight to fight or to survive – there are even people who fight to keep themselves going. So, people's motivation for doing certain things is indeed as varied as their consciousnesses.

People's different approach to life and their environment is e.g. clearly expressed when several people, who live in the same street, pass a certain neighbour's house:

One person might be happy that spring has finally arrived and that the trees have come into leaf. This individual sees colours full of life everywhere and small, hopeful flowers popping out of the earth where the lawn has not been mowed. This individual's focus is thus on the presence of life and joy.

Another individual might immediately point out that the lawn needs to be mowed in this particular yard, and that the garden shed needs painting. This individual, who is obviously a neat person, does not know how to relax and enjoy the arrival of spring because a neighbour does not keep his yard as neat as this individual does himself.

A neighbour down the street might enjoy the sound of children playing in the yard, because this individual loves children. Another neighbour, however, might get annoyed that the children are noisy once again, because he or she has bad experience with children and finds them distracting.

I could go on and on about people's different perspectives on the same situation, based on their different backgrounds, upbringing, life experience, convictions, beliefs and basic human values.

Since it is so difficult to satisfy several people at the same time, you might as well decide to just satisfy yourself, with a high consideration for your immediate environment and for the Earth as a whole by, e.g. being environmentally conscious. In doing so, we consider the Crystal Energy, which takes the individual as well as the wholeness into account, and thereby planet Earth at the same time. In addition, we must show respect for the presence of human views that are different from our own, as long as these have a human perspective, even though we may not agree with those outlooks on life and those ideologies at all.

A great capacity for being humane, consciousness, acceptance and flexibility – these are the determining qualities for Crystal Humans' relationships with one another, even if people are fundamentally different in nature.

The Crystal Human

A Crystal Human is a human without an ego. Instead, a Crystal Human has a 'self' or an 'I', from which the individual defines him or herself. Crystal Children of our time and of the future are thus all born with an 'I' and know nothing about having an ego.

When adults have their aura transformed into a Crystal aura through an AuraTransformation™ and when they fully crystallize in their bodies, their former ego also completely disappears, if indeed they had one previously.

During the Aura and Body Crystallization Process, the frequency and spiritual enlightenment is increased in the Soul and Indigo Humans to such an extent that their physical ego simply ceases to exist. As a result of the increase in frequency and the spiritual enlightenment that occurs during the Crystallization Phase, in the physical aura as well as the physical body structure, an 'I' will appear instead. The 'I' enables all Crystal Humans to act as balanced individuals with a constant focus on the respective spiritual and physical aspects of life, at the same time.

When extremely spiritual people are aura transformed – i.e. people who their entire lives found it difficult to define themselves in earthly terms - their energies are gathered in the aura at first and then in their bodies. Through this process, they are individualized and create an 'I', from which they can begin to define and express themselves. Some call it grounding, but in reality the people in question are coming alive as human individuals in the earthly universe, by becoming fully present in their physical bodies and their spiritual consciousness.

Simply put – when a person is crystallized in his or her aura and body, which happens when the individual moves through the four elements of Fire, Water, Earth and Air of the 5th- 8th dimensions, that individual becomes a Crystal Human of the 9th dimension with a fully integrated 'I' consciousness. An 'I' consciousness is one that is based on the presence of the four elements of Fire, Water, Earth and Air in the individual's energy.

In the 9th dimension, the individual identifies his or her Crystal life mission, hidden deep within the cell structure of their physical body. This happens when the Spiritual Energy in the aura penetrates and enlightens each cell in the individual's body, thus transforming them into Crystal cells and activating the individual's life mission.

In relation to the Crystal Human living out their Crystal life mission that appeared in the 9th dimension, he or she begins to crystallize into their social and consciousness network by integrating the four elements, which leads to the individual building up a Crystal network around them. This network Crystallization happens from the 9th-12th dimension making the Crystal Human more holistic at all levels, thus gradually transforming them into a Crystal Human of the 13th dimension.

I will elaborate on the four elements and the energies of the 5th-8th dimensions at a later point in the book, but I would like to point out, at this stage, that it is important to distinguish between being fully crystallized as a Crystal Individual of the 9th dimension and being a fully crystallized Crystal Human of the 13th dimension.

This book focuses on the Crystal Human as well as the Crystallization Process as a way to become a fully Crystallized Human of the 13th dimension and it is therefore vital that you, the reader, understand that most newborn babies, who are born in 2009 and in the years up until 2012-13, are at a Crystal Individual level of the 9th dimension and therefore not yet complete Crystal Humans of the 13th dimension. Adult aura-transformed people, however, are somewhere between the Indigo Energy of the 4th dimension and the Crystal Individual Energy of the 9th dimension. With this, I hope to avoid any misunderstandings, as the Crystal Individual and Crystal Human terms are quite similar.

Returning to the more down-to-earth part of the topic, however, the completely transparent, sparkly pink-violet Crystal aura is not nearly as pronounced as the dark, deep-blue Indigo aura. However, at consciousness level, the Crystal aura has a much stronger energy structure than the Indigo aura, because the Crystal aura is completely impenetrable from outside energies that do not match Crystal Humans' inner consciousness balance. It is therefore pretty much impossible to entice Crystal Humans, if the individual does not want this, because first and foremost, he or she follows their own intuition, rather than external impulses.

The Crystal aura contains both the physically visible, as well as the spiritually invisible, spectra at the same time. This enables Crystal Humans to either be fully visible to everyone at a consciousness level, or to be consciously completely invisible to the outside world, so that others forget to think about them altogether.

When a Crystal Human activates the spiritual, invisible part of their charisma in relation to the outside world, the environment becomes completely incapable of picking up their signals – pretty much as if they were dead and had left the sphere of the Earth – which must be considered to be a big advantage for well-known Crystal Humans in particular, when they need peace and quiet away from the public eye and the media from time to time. The media, without even thinking why, then shifts their focus to others.

If a Crystal Human wishes to burn through to the outside world in a strong way, this person may then choose to focus on the more physical part of their Crystal aura and therefore outshine the environment with the sparkling facets of their 'personal diamond'.

However, if several Crystal Humans are present in the same room, they always choose to shine together without competing for first place, as there is no such thing as a first place in a multifaceted diamond (crystal), which occurs when several Crystal Humans stay or work together. You see, there would be no diamond if it were not for the many facets that are present at the same time. A diamond therefore represents a wholeness consisting of several different facets that, together, create the play of energies that makes the diamond sparkle..

Characteristics of a Crystal Human at the human level include being very focused and balanced with a great inner strength and a good connection with their inner voice. Their external, personal expression is completely in balance with their inner core essence. They are very aware of their individual platform in life and they know that there is only one person like him or herself and that no two individuals in the earthly matrix are the same.

At the same time they have an inner, clear consciousness that, once all future Crystal Humans find their own individual platform in the earthly matrix, the Earth's energy will start to shine like a large diamond (crystal) with its many different facets as one wholeness, which is the objective of the Crystal Energy.

Crystal Humans have good intuition while being good at reading other people's body language, which makes them bilingual and equally good at reading the internal and external human languages. They appear as deeply harmonious people with a good perspective, and generally they are very content by nature. If they are unhappy with something, they immediately try to change it, thinking of others as much as themselves, because Crystal Humans always think of the wholeness as much as the individual.

As for consciousness, Crystal Humans arrive on Earth via the Venus route when they are born, since the Venus route is the consciousness birth route with the highest frequency leading to our planet when coming from our own solar system. This is the route that most newborn babies nowadays take, as the energy matches the Earth's future, spiritual development stage in every way.

From the mid 1990's up until 2009 it has only been possible for Indigos to arrive here via the Jupiter route, which is a highway with extraordinarily wide lanes. In the period from 2009 to 2012-13, there will be two main routes, or rather highways, to choose from, as both Jupiter and Venus have birth ways to the Earth.

Up until the Indigo period from the mid 1990's, when the Earth was exclusively at Soul level, you could, however, arrive here directly from any of the planets in our solar system. This meant that you were born with an energy structure and consciousness qualities corresponding to those on the planet that you arrived from. What characterized all individuals who arrived here on Earth, though, was that – prior to being physically born – they had been equipped with a blueprint from the Moon and the Akashic Records indicating each Soul's individual path of life and destiny here on Earth. The consciousness blueprint that originated from the Akashic Records gave them the advance knowledge of their respective place in the earthly reincarnation system.

All those individuals who, during the time of Soul consciousness, arrived here from other solar systems in which there was no knowledge of Soul Energy, had to use the exact same consciousness approaches to Earth as those used by the solar system's own inhabitants. So, on their way here, they stopped at one or more of the planets within the solar system in order to be introduced to the physical Soul Energy as well as the reincarnation structure on this planet. It is therefore possible to register familiar planet energy impulses from our own solar system from time to time, in a Pleiades or Sirius human's consciousness, since these planet energies represent the spiritual Pleiades or Sirius human's physically dense influence on the individual's route towards Earth. You can read more about this in my book 'The Planet Energies Behind the Earth's Population 2005' ('Planetenergierne bag Jordens befolkning 2005' - currently available in Danish only).

When the Indigo Energy made it through to Earth in the mid 1980's, with its divided and yet balanced Spiritual and Physical Energy, this happened through an expansion of the main consciousness route from Jupiter, which is home to the characteristics of a strong, spiritual insight combined with a powerful and physically manifesting energy.

This main route was always there on equal terms with the other main roads from the Sun, the Moon, Mercury, Mars, Venus, Saturn, Uranus, Neptune and Pluto, respectively. However, not in the same wide-lane version as it is today.

In 1995 Jupiter took over full control of the consciousness influx to Earth, which is why the Indigo route was expanded to a 10-lane highway in order to accommodate the entire dissemination of newborn babies to the Earth.

In 2012, the Earth's full consciousness management will be transferred from Jupiter to Venus, which represents a higher-frequency consciousness gateway with contact to many other universes out there, not only in this solar system.

In consciousness contexts, Venus can be seen as a very holistic planet, but with a strong focus on each individual. As other planets in our solar system increase their consciousness frequency to match the spiritual frequency of the Venus Crystal Energy, they will similarly assert themselves as gateways for Crystal Humans and other future New Time Humans to arrive on Earth. We will see much more of this when the new Golden Energy, at some point in future, really starts to materialize here on Earth, in its firm and yet flexible and intelligent form.

Case

"Kom mai du skjønne milde!"

(Song title: "Come May, wonderful and mild!")

By Aura Mediator™ Kristian Fredheim, a 45-year-old man from Norway:

It happened in May, that which I had been waiting to understand all my life!

Today, I am extremely happy that I completed the transformation that I needed in order to get on with my life. At first, my body reacted as if it had acquired the balance it needed - a balance that released all ties and which left a sense of being that made me feel good. As a person, I have been particularly good at *beating around the bush*. This quality was for me transformed from being *unclear* to becoming very *clear*. My senses were sharpened and it felt like I was able to open up to 'the entire world'. This was one of the main reasons why I decided to undergo my AuraTransformation™. I wanted to become more visible and I wanted to sharpen my senses, so that I could realize my life mission. My life mission is to make people aware of their potential and I need to be a good communicator in order to do that. In addition, it was essential for me to get rid of my old *ties*.

At first, I didn't have any physical problems, but I sensed a change that felt like a kind of *fermentation*. At the same time, my body entered into a phase where my performance seemed a bit unstable and strange. My body felt worn, as if it had difficulty receiving all the light that it needed. I practice inner exercises from the revitalization Tao. These exercises have been of great benefit to me and I can highly recommend them. I have adjusted the exercises to fit into my own, daily ritual of approximately 20 minutes.

The pain that started about six months after the transformation was primarily centered around my pelvis and my lower back. I was prepared for the pain but not for such an accelerated sense of aging. My Master of Taekwondo asked me, "Did you turn 81?" As you can imagine, I could have lived without that experience and without the lack of mobility. It is deeply unsatisfying when every little thing is a struggle, such as putting on your socks and shoes. During this time, I also saw a reflexologist, who massaged me with oils to increase the blood circulation in my back. The effect would last for a day or two, and then I would be back to square one.

Anni Sennov told me to stop the treatments, simply to give the AuraTrans-formation™ room to find its place. She also recommended that I take OPC BARK capsules (pine bark) and the herbal supplement Life Spice® Vital, which contains 31 different herbs, spices and roots. That did it for me and right away it felt like the entire process stabilized within my body. To go from being 81 years old to 45 is an incredible feeling when your mobility and flexibility have been pressed to the extreme. After that I increased my intake of vitamin B and this contributed to my vitality and my overall well-being as well. My vitamin C requirement decreased from 1-3 mg per day to 1-3 mg per week. My diet is regular and can be described as typical Norwegian. I usually eat a lot of vegetables in addition to beef, poultry and fish.

My biggest milestones after the transformation have been the completion of my book, 'Master of the Moment – The Key to Your Lifeline' ('Øyeblikkets Mester – nøkkelen til livslinjen' - available in Norwegian only), and the fact that I am now living on my own. There was simply not enough space in my life to allow for my life mission the way I used to live - this resulted in me completing seven years of writing, three months after the transformation.

I experienced that the things, which had been building up in my life were now clarified. My partner and I, who were living together, were familiar with the usual challenges of any relationship; still, I experienced that I became less patient while my boundaries became clearer. This resulted in an end to our six-year relationship, four months after my transformation. My Dharma became clearer and clearer and showed me that I needed to open doors, rather than feeling like a 'doormat'. Not that anyone has ever called me that, but I felt that the time had come to realize 'something' greater than myself, which required my full attention!

When my friends ask me how it was and how I'm doing, I say, "If I had dreamed of ending my relationship 'properly', I would have done it the same way we did! We are great friends and really like each other, the only problem is that we are on two different planets, which is why it is better for us to live apart! I know that she is just as happy where she is as I am where I am!"

My mood was quite good and I felt grateful. Grateful to Anni Sennov as my main source of knowledge and not least to my two mentors, International Director Berit Reaver and Instructor Henriette Gustavsen, from The Aura Mediator Courses™ in Norway, who completed my transformation and prepared everything for me to become an Aura Mediator™.

Before my AuraTransformation™, my automatic pattern of thoughts would take me back and forth in a way that made it difficult for me to complete what I needed to do. After the transformation I was able to complete everything I had dreamed of completing. I was able to take care of everything that had had to wait, and my life took on a meaning. My list of things to do is almost gone and I am expecting much fewer challenges in the future. My conscience is thus much better and I am so thankful.

In closing I would like to repeat the message I sent to my mentors when everything had melded together and my heart became whole on May 27, 2008 at 10:27 (five days after I became an Aura Mediator™):

"Hi Berit. Today, I balanced in the sunshine. I paid thanks and meditated, did my inner exercises and then connected with my inner self in order to feel the oneness. All the birds were singing, some louder than others, everyone was there and when the sound was at it loudest, the three chakras melded together as one. My heart was filled with light and I became one with everything. Thank you so much to you and Henriette for helping make this happen!"

- and to you, who have been aura transformed, and are still waiting for the light to reach you, I say, "You must let go of the ties that bind you to gain access to the light that is awaiting you." Your intention determines the rest! Good luck!

"THE OLD, THE INDIGO AND THE CRYSTAL"

The aura's journey from Soul to Crystal Energy

So now that you have some insight into the essence of the Crystal Human, it is perhaps appropriate to take a look back at the early days of Soul Consciousness. During this time the Crystal Energy worked hard, using a variety of consciousness-expanding methods, some of them 'back door', to break through the aura of those many adults who matched the Crystal Energy at consciousness level at that time.

However, it was not as easy for the Crystal Energy to gain access to people's consciousness here on Earth as you might think. Although back then, many people were wholeheartedly interested in spirituality, the Soul aura was not designed such that the Spirit was easily accessible in everyday life. You see, in order to connect with your spiritual consciousness, you had to travel all the way to the other side of the etheric body, the astral body and the Lower Mental Body in order to continue on to your Higher Mental Energy. For many people, this was a very long journey into consciousness.

You therefore had limited options of getting close to the spirit, and this was either through: near-death experience; through the use of consciousness-expanding drugs; or through meditation, which many Oriental people have practiced for thousands of years. You could also take an astral trip into your physical consciousness on the astral planes, but this had nothing to do with pure Spiritual Energy, as we know it from the Crystal Energy today. So in reality, that route did not work, even though many people thought they were on the right path. It did, on the other hand, provide a physical taste of the timeless condition, which the Spiritual Energy represents in all humans.

If it had been that easy for Soul Humans to transform their Soul aura to a spiritually based Crystal aura on their own, today there would definitely be more aura-transformed people here on Earth than is the case. But why is it not possible for a person to transform his or her own aura without the help of an Aura Mediator™ who practises AuraTransformation™?

When you have a Soul aura you can easily attract New Time Indigo and Crystal Energies in your consciousness by yourself. However, when your consciousness needs to be expanded, which happens through an AuraTransformation™, you have to let go of all your dense Soul Energy, which was up until now tied into your aura around your physical body. This allows the energy to gather in some lighter energy layers of a higher frequency in your aura.

You actually die a little in order to make a rebirth possible at consciousness level. This little death occurs when your aura is transformed from Soul to Indigo or Crystal Energy, and the Aura Mediator™ helps you maintain consciousness contact with your body during the transformation.

When you let go of all your dense physicality in the Soul aura, which helps you stay grounded because of its direct contact with your physical body, it is like letting go of an air balloon with too much fuel, i.e. Spiritual Energy, onboard.

Once you have let go of your air balloon, i.e. your soul-based physicality, in order for it to be transformed into a new consciousness structure consisting of a more spiritual Indigo or Crystal aura, you must remain grounded at the same time. This is of course impossible if you let go of your air balloon while being onboard yourself - because no physical being is able to stand on the Earth and steer their air balloon while floating around in it up in the air. This is physically impossible as well as impossible from a consciousness perspective.

If no Aura Mediator™ was present during the transformation situation to maintain body contact and grounding for you, your life would end up being one long fight to attract the new Indigo and Crystal Energies. Yet, at the same time, you would be struggling to stay connected to your experience on the physical, earthly dimension and maintain a relationship with your fellow humans and your physical body. It is extremely difficult to maintain an inner balance simply because it is not possible to have direct contact both with Earth and Heaven, the body and the spirit, at the same time, unless you possess an aura that connects the two worlds and consciousnesses. It is this aura that the Aura Mediator™ helps you gather at Spiritual level, after it has been loosened at the Soul level.

An Aura Mediator™ is a practitioner who is trained to carry out AuraTransformations on their clients, providing help in both transforming and upgrading the aura from Soul to Indigo or Crystal level. An Aura Mediator™ possesses the power and physicality necessary to do this, while at the same time also containing light and Spirit integrated in a balanced way within his or her personal consciousness.

The Aura Mediator™ is also trained to act as a facilitator for the client and acts as the client's physical grounding while the client is trying to establish his or her full spiritual consciousness. The Aura Mediator™ simply ensures a tight hold on the air balloon and thus to the client's energy during the process. The Aura Mediator™ ensures that the client moves through this ascension process in a balanced way and re-establishes a good connection with his or her physical body.

If you try to integrate the Indigo and the Crystal Energies into the Soul aura in large doses, without first completely letting go of the physical Soul aura structure, you will quickly develop claustrophobia within your own consciousness. This will cause the old energy bodies in the Soul aura to automatically let go of their ties to the body and you will subsequently be left with a feeling of being in no man's land. This is the general experience of clients that our instructors and I, as well as many other trained Aura Mediators have come across, who tried to transform their Soul auras into an Indigo or Crystal aura by themselves. This we definitely do not recommend.

So far, I have yet to hear about a single incident when a person succeeded in performing an AuraTransformation™ on him or herself. Once an AuraTransformation™ has been performed through a trained Aura Mediator™, all have agreed that you cannot at all compare the two conditions before and after the AuraTransformation™.

Through an AuraTransformation™ you become aware of your own consciousness, enabling you to better relate to your own potential. At the same time, you gain a greater insight into your Spiritual Energy within your aura and your own personal charisma, which is visible to others on the earthly stage in the physical world.

The Aura Mediator™, who is already in the outer earthly and physically dense world with his or her full spiritual potential visible to themselves and others, helps their clients get past the stage curtain, figuratively speaking, so that they all end up on the stage in the physical world, rather than behind in the spiritual and partially invisible world.

When the Spirit no longer finds enough breathing space within the physical Soul Energy, and the claustrophobic feeling deep inside becomes too big, it is time to undergo an AuraTransformation™.

Most Soul Individuals experience this when it is time to have their aura transformed from Soul to Spiritual level - a feeling that, in many ways, corresponds to young people gradually feeling the need to leave their childhood home, as they become more adult and independent.

Most people with a primary focus on physical energy and the physical aspect of their lives often follow the overall Spiritual plan that has been made for their earthly lives, without questioning the process. They have an innate acceptance of life and of the fact that physicality has its own fundamental limitations. In addition, they view physical death as a natural end to life.

It can be difficult to inspire physically oriented people into undergoing a transformation of their consciousness towards the Crystal Energy, if there are no strong incentives for this in their physical lives. Physically oriented people therefore often need to have a specific reason for deciding to undergo a consciousness transformation in their lives, before opening up to the idea that there is in fact more to life than what you can see, hear, feel, smell and taste.

It is often only when exposed to lay-offs, divorce, personal illness or illness within their immediate family, death in the family or among close friends, or until they are in an accident, that they slowly start to feel and/or acknowledge the need to see the world and themselves from a bigger perspective, in order to understand, if at all possible, why they were exposed to these difficult experiences. Some acknowledge that they need to become balanced and increase their vibration, which incidentally is rarely how they would express themselves, in order to adjust to a new consciousness platform at a more advanced level.

The need for an AuraTransformation™ may also occur when people suddenly experience something incomprehensible, inexplicable or supernatural, which cannot be explained satisfactorily from an earthly, physical perspective. Last, but not least, it may occur if they suddenly experience physical or psychological emptiness in their lives, such as depression, etc.

Fortunately, when physically oriented people have a sense of emptiness in their lives because they are out of touch with their own Spiritual Energy and life impulse, they are often easily motivated to undergoing an AuraTransformation™. This is because they prefer specific solutions to specific problems and pointlessness and emptiness are very tangible problems for them, which can often be easily rectified through an AuraTransformation™.

If the Spirit has already made its way into your body before you undergo an AuraTransformation™, and your Spiritual Energy is in the process of becoming integrated into your body's cell structure, or it is in the process of overwriting your body's cell memory – and your body, and your brain in particular, cannot keep up with the new, high frequencies – this often manifests itself in various ways. Below is a list of physical symptoms that are often related to the Spirit's need for becoming integrated into the aura and the body in a balanced way through an AuraTransformation™. These occur simply because the Soul Energy is no longer capable of keeping the pure spiritual impulse out of its physically dense energy structure in the aura as well as the body:

- Light sensitivity and burning or red eyes

- Shortness of breath and asthma-like symptoms

- Flu-like symptoms as well as pain in joints, bones, body aches associated with fever, which antibiotics do not alleviate

- Itchy rash, eczema and sudden onset of allergies and hay fever

- Runny nose and sneezing when changing from warm to cold temperatures, or vice versa

- Sore throat with no sign of viral or bacterial infection

- Ringing in the ears and tinnitus

- Dizziness, fatigue and exhaustion – appearing out of nowhere

- Insomnia and/or increased need for more sleep than usual. Sleep does not regulate itself properly

- Migraine-like headache that does not respond to painkillers

The above examples are taken from my book, 'Crystal Children, Indigo Children & Adults of the Future'.

Last, but not least, today many adult Soul Humans are motivated to have their personal energies upgraded to Indigo or Crystal level, to better allow them to keep up with their beloved children's high-frequency energy levels.

This is particularly the case for those parents of hyperactive and/or problematic Indigo Children possibly with ADHD, ADD, etc. who love to turn the world upside down in order to wake up their parents and other adults from their slumbering spiritual consciousness. These children will apply any methods they need in order for this to happen. Usually there is nothing that parents will not do to better understand their beloved and perhaps challenging children.

I could go on for hours about the transition from Soul to Spiritual Energy and elaborate on why and how, etc., but to round off this chapter in a clean and simple way, I have chosen to bring the following case that was written by the Norwegian Aura Mediator™, Anne Grethe Brandsøy. Anne Grethe describes some common conditions that apply to the majority of people, who have had their Soul aura or the remnants thereof upgraded to an Indigo or Crystal aura through an AuraTransformation™.

Case

Aura Mediator™, Anne Grethe Brandsøy, a 44-year-old woman from Western Norway describes how she personally benefited from her AuraTransformation™:

Since 1992 when I became a massage therapist, I have worked with personal development. I worked part-time as a massage therapist up until 2001 when massage therapy and other forms of therapy became my full-time occupation. I have organized and participated in many courses on personal development and health in the years since then. It has been very fulfilling and interesting, but also a lot of hard work. I often experienced that the same problems came up time after time.

In the spring of 2006 I participated in an Alternative Health Fair in Bergen, Norway, and listened to Anni Sennov and Berit Reaver (Director for The Aura Mediator Courses™ internationally) talk about AuraTransformation™. I found it extremely interesting. If this new form of treatment lived up to its promise, I would be able to get help with the challenges I had been facing for many years.

The following summer I underwent my AuraTransformation™ and can testify that it has fulfilled all my wishes – in fact, so much that I became a certified Aura Mediator™ in June 2007.

Below is a description of some of the effects the transformation had on me:

PHYSICALLY:

A sense of well-being in my body:
Immediately upon my AuraTransformation™ I felt an enormous sense of well-being in my body – sort of like a calm flow of wonderful energy. Previously, I had only come close to this depth of feeling on a very few occasions, such as after a week of rest and recuperation involving meditation and deep treatments.

A sense of presence in my body:
I am much more present in my body now than I used to be. Before, I was only more present in my mind. I also feel that my body is much more 'grounded'. I live more in the moment.

The energy is more gathered:
I feel more whole inside my body and my Rose and massage therapists have commented that my energy seems to be more gathered and whole, and the imbalances in my aura are now gone.

My body is warmer:
I have a better energy flow in my body and my legs don't get cold as easily as they used to. My hands feel warmer.

My senses are sharpened:
I particularly feel that my sense of touch has been sharpened – including both physical touch and when I work with the energy field around others. It is now easier for me to feel the energies of the clients I massage and to locate the problem(s) in their body. My body also gives clearer signals when something is good or bad.

My body is stronger:
I have better strength and endurance and I feel this for example when I go for a walk in the forest, where I usually walk the same route in steep, hilly terrain. Since my AuraTransformation™ I can handle the gradients much more easily than I used to, even if it has been a long time since I walked the route. I am also stronger when I massage now and don't get physically tired as quickly as I used to.

My body lets me know:
My body lets me know clearly e.g. when I need food, rest or exercise. Fortunately, I also feel it when these needs have been met.
When I am especially busy, my body tells me to stop when it is tired. If I do not listen to the message, I get very tired and get a general feeling of weakness. My voice loses its strength and my eyes and my balance are

weakened as well.

I used to ignore my body's signals for longer periods of time, but I don't think that's very smart in the long run as that only leads to overloading of my system and can cause serious infirmities or illness.

PSYCHOLOGICALLY:

Emotionally stronger:
I can handle more emotional stress than I used to – I don't freak out over little things and am better at handling bigger things – and more calmly.

I get less stressed out:
I have a deep, inner calm and take things as they come. I don't feel the need to spend a long time preparing for meetings and other things that used to stress me out days ahead of time. Although, I still prepare what is necessary in time.

Love for others:
I often feel content and happy and also appreciate more those people around me.

I have more courage to confront others:
I am now no longer afraid to deal with uncomfortable topics early on. I used to push problems aside to the extent that they would pile up and become extremely uncomfortable to have to discuss with someone.

Increased self-worth:
I used to need affirmation all the time, and in my eyes, I was never good enough, no matter how much affirmation I got.

Affirmation is no longer important to me, although naturally it is nice when I get complimented for my efforts, but I no longer feel a 'need' for affirmation and praise. I know when I have done a good job and am happy for others and myself.

My own self has been strengthened:
I no longer put up with being treated poorly or degraded by others. It is

now easier for me to put my foot down, without fearing people's reaction.

MENTALLY AND SPIRITUALLY:

I have a clearer mind:
I am quicker at reasoning. It is as if my 'hard disk' has been cleaned up and now has much more room. My thoughts are clearer.

My intuition is strengthened:
I get clearer messages regarding big and small things, e.g. I often know the answer to something during a conversation. My telepathy has also been strengthened.

I find it easier to make choices:
I used to be very torn when having to make decisions – should I be rational, should I listen to previous experience or should I let my heart decide for me? – Or should society and my upbringing have the last word? Since my AuraTransformation™ I feel that it is now much easier to know what is right for me.

If I have made a wrong decision or gone in the wrong direction, I get physically and mentally tired, but I then get re-energized when I change my course towards the right direction. The Universe seems to cooperate when I make the right choices.

My dreams are clearer:
Even the messages and the symbolism in my dreams.

I turn ideas into action:
I now manage to turn ideas and thoughts into action, often those things that I have been wanting to do and have been postponing for a long time. This can be for the fun, but also for the more boring but necessary, activities.

I am happy with life:
I am generally much happier with life and am no longer afraid and scared of sinister things that might happen, I believe more that whatever happens is right for me. I mostly enjoy a good flow and I'm in balance with

my environment.

I connect better with children:
I meet children in a totally different and more direct way. Our dialogs are more open and honest.
It is easier to set boundaries and explain things to children. Everybody seems happier.

Personal development:
I no longer feel the need to attend courses and groups on personal development. I have tried it a few times since my AuraTransformation™, but in a way I felt that I was done with the topics that were discussed and that I no longer needed to go back and retrieve old traumas. Even group exercises that were supposed to help me were a big mistake for me. I became completely exhausted and unbalanced for a long time after. This was early on after my AuraTransformation™ and I had yet to learn the techniques that would help me regain my balance much quicker.
I still need to work on my old patterns of thought and action, but in a different way. The rather large, fundamental problems that I have been struggling with all these years have resurfaced, and I work on this myself and also get help from an Aura Mediator™ or another type of therapist, e.g. a Kinesiologist. However, I feel that it is easier to understand and change my 'problems' now since my AuraTransformation™. The process is faster and not as exhausting and, more importantly, I deal with the problems once and for all.

Healing:
I no longer feel the need to receive healing from someone who has not undergone an AuraTransformation™. I feel that the energies do not match and it feels somewhat uncomfortable. I have tried colour therapy with the same effect.

The aura's journey from Indigo to Crystal Energy

These days, the Crystal Energy is integrated more and more into societies around the world, which is particularly reflected in the technological development that in many ways follows the Earth's general consciousness development. However, not everyone supports the implementation of new technology at home and on the job, and similarly, not everyone supports the integration of new consciousness in their auras and bodies. This is a fact that aura-transformed individuals in particular, who have consciously chosen to take a full step into the New Time with the energy of their entire being, may have to accept. Not everyone extols the presence of Spirit in matter in the same way as aura-transformed individuals – that is just how it is.

Not everyone finds it easy to live with a great degree of transparency and openness in their personal life processes. This means of course that everybody around them is able to clearly see, sense or in other ways acknowledge the scope of their consciousness as well as the extent of their commitment to a certain cause, or lack thereof.

As a deeply spiritual individual at Crystal level you must, as a new aspect of life, take your hands out of your pockets and show what you can do at the physical level in life, which may not be one of your strengths. Correspondingly, as a physically oriented individual, you must now base your life on close, human values and unity of consciousness, which may not be one of your strengths, either. This is indeed a new, never-before-seen and exciting combination. A combination that is finding its way to the surface of the Earth where people are guaranteed to feel insecure more than once during the particular integration processes.

With the transition from Soul to Indigo Energy and on into pure Spiritual Energy at Crystal level, the Crystal Energy prepares the groundwork for all adults to develop beyond their existing physical, consciousness platform, in order for them to become whole beings or physically incarnated spiritual beings, if you wish.

Indigo Children of our time will also have to travel part of this way to become completely pure spiritual beings, whereas Crystal Children entirely avoid this process, as they already have an innate pure Spiritual Energy fully integrated into their auras and physical bodies.

During the physical-spiritual fusion process, i.e. the Crystallization Process, the AuraTransformation™ acts as a physical key to activating the Crystallization Process in the aura, which at the Soul and Indigo levels, respectively, has a much lighter energy structure than that of the physical body. On the other hand, at Crystal level, the aura's frequency completely matches that of the body, which many spiritual people, who have yet to undergo an AuraTransformation™, may find hard to imagine. This suggests how physically strong and impenetrable a Crystal aura really is, once it has fully crystallized on par with the body, because it is completely impenetrable to all external energies and conditions that the Crystal Human chooses not to let into his or her personal universe. Correspondingly, the Crystal aura is very open to anything new that is positive or progressive in nature. This is a distinctive process of inner as well as external character, which, for fully Crystallized Humans, takes place continuously at cell level within the physical Crystal body and, which is controlled with an iron fist by the Crystal Human's deep balance-oriented consciousness.

Similarly, the fact that the frequency in the aura and the body completely match at Crystal level shows how much lighter the frequency of a Crystal body is compared to that of a Soul and Indigo-controlled body. However, it is far from easy to crystallize your body, as this is a long, radical process both physically and from a consciousness perspective.

In contrast to the Aura Crystallization, which can be initiated through an AuraTransformation™, the Body Crystallization can happen completely independently of the Aura Crystallization, which I will elaborate in the main chapter, 'Body Crystallization', in *'The Crystal Human and the Crystallization Process Part II'*.

Simply put, a fully crystallized human's aura is like the yard around the house that people tend not to go into, unless they have personal business there. Looking at it this way, the environment has the opportunity to get advance insight into the energy of the person's inner being, because the aura acts as an expanded sphere of intimacy. The body therefore acts as the house itself where not everybody can look in and where the particular person lives with the majority of his or her Spiritual Energy.

The body acts as a physical storage room for the Crystal Energy, while being used as a tool for registration in the earthly sphere and the daily environment.

Contrary to this, the aura acts as a consciousness shield and energy radar that enables the individual to register external moods, thoughts, trends and information of subtler and more intuitive nature, that have yet to find their way to the person on a physical level.

Correspondingly, others can also register energies and thoughts, etc. that the individual has yet to announce to the outside world. Through the aura, it is also possible to register information and input from the invisible part of the earthly sphere as well as from other planets and unknown states of consciousness around the Universe.

Returning to the simple house/yard symbolism, you meet with some people to have a chat on the sidewalk, outside your house or in your yard. Others, you invite inside for a cup of coffee on the patio in the backyard showing a slightly greater will and openness to connect with those people. Others, you choose to invite inside your house for coffee or dinner because you wish to have those people become more involved in your life.

Transforming from Indigo to Crystal level is a process that all Indigo Children and aura-transformed Indigo Adults can do without necessarily getting consciousness support from an Aura Mediator™. However, it is helpful for most people to have some knowledge about the Crystallization Process as well as understanding the reason behind the process, to achieve the best possible cooperation from the Indigo system – which is the reason I decided to write 'The Crystal Human and the Crystallization Process Part I' and 'Part II'.

The pure Indigo Energy's influence on people's personal expression and their everyday lives is described in my previous book, 'Balance at All Levels' ('Balance på alle planer' - available in Danish only) of 2002, which is a development and rewriting of the book 'The New Aura' ('Den nye aura') of 2001 which, again, is an extension of the booklet 'The Aura Transformation's ABC' ('Aura-ændringens ABC') of 1999.

Rather than repeating myself in this book, I will focus on selected aspects that are relevant for the transition from the Indigo to the Crystal Energy.

Indigo Humans all have a strong, magnetic dark blue-violet and Indigo-coloured Balancing Body in their aura, which is the part of the aura that has lent its name to the term 'Indigo Human'. In addition, these people possess tons of pure Spiritual Energy in their aura beyond the Balancing Body, which is able to communicate with the body's energy through the Indigo-coloured Balancing Body. The Balancing Body thus acts as an interpreter between the Spirit and the body and is capable of expressing itself in two different languages, i.e. the body language and the spiritual language.

When the time comes for Indigo Humans to become crystallized, their

Crystallization Process simply aims at melding together the two separate communication systems – the spiritual system and the body system – into one combined system, so that communication is no longer required through an interpreter, i.e. the Balancing Body. The Crystallization Process aims to transform the large amount of Spiritual Energy that lies within the aura outside the Balancing Body so that, instead, it will find its way into the Indigo-coloured Balancing Body as well as the body itself, both of which will result in an increase in vibratory level.

As a result of the Crystallization Process, the Balancing Body therefore is the only part of the aura that remains, once the Spiritual Energy is fully and completely integrated into the visible aura close to the body as well as in the actual body. When this happens, the aura changes from acting as a protective, magnetic Balancing Body to an expanded Crystal intimacy sphere instead. An intimacy sphere that does not seem as pronounced and substantial as the Balancing Body in the Indigo aura, but one that is especially noticeable when the Crystal Individual is in a long queue at the grocery store and can easily think his or her own thoughts without being distracted by other people's talk and thoughts. In a situation like that, the Crystal aura really does itself justice.

During the Crystallization Phase the aura changes its colour and structure from a strong, magnetic Indigo-coloured force to a paler pink-violet crystal-like diamond with a crystal-clear and visibly shining radiation. However, do not be fooled into believing that the Crystal Energy is weak and fragile compared to the Indigo Energy, as this is not the case at all. On the contrary, it is hard as a cut diamond and carries a strong spiritual coding regarding what is right and what is wrong in every context in relation to the individual. A state of truth that, during the Body Crystallization, finds its way into the body all the way down to cell level, after which the individual feels the need to act out their inner truth, as they would otherwise be committing an offence against themselves.

When changing from the Indigo to the Crystal Energy, everybody starts to take much more personal responsibility and perceive their own consciousness and physical situation much clearer than ever before - even if they were very responsible during the Indigo Phase. No matter how they used to view themselves in relation to the world before, they will now start to view the world from many more angles simultaneously, just like viewing a finely facetted diamond.

The great big world gradually opens up more and more to people with Indigo Energy who are in the process of becoming crystallized, with the exception of the long periods of time, however, when the Body Crystallization is taking place, when they automatically need more rest. This is why it becomes a very important part of the personal puzzle for fully crystallized people to be in touch with many and very different types of people in their everyday lives, and preferably also globally.

Many physical networks that are based on common interests and affiliations as well as the numerous social networks through the Internet will continue to grow substantially over the coming decades. It is then the Crystal Humans' turn to make a positive difference on Earth with the purpose of leading the Spiritual Energy right down into the earthly matter.

Today, all babies are born with the Spiritual Energy fully integrated into their bodies, which is why the Crystal Energy is a completely natural and congenital consciousness condition for them, and these children are guaranteed to build up social networks through the Internet and in society already at a very young age.

For the majority of adults, especially those with Soul Energy, and partially those with Indigo Energy, it is, however, a brand new experience to be networking with people they do not know at all well. In the coming years, however, networking will create the foundation for brand new opportunities and the possibility for different types of experiences in their personal lives. These experiences will again expand their insight and perspectives and break down personal boundaries that may no longer be relevant in their lives.

No more channelling

Many Indigo Humans experience that, regardless of their age, they can easily manage the part of their personal energy that is within the Balancing Body in their aura. However, due to the fact that their physical body is constantly moving backwards and forwards across the bridge between the joint consciousness at Soul Level, and the pure Spiritual Energy in the aura outside their own Balancing Body, they are at risk of becoming disoriented from time to time, when communicating with the outside world. It is sometimes difficult for them to figure out when to speak the language of the Spirit and the language of the body, which at Soul level are diametrically opposite, while at Crystal level they are completely identical?

At Crystal level all form of communication becomes much easier for everyone, as the two languages (Spirit and Body) have been brought together and integrated within the aura as well as the body. Then, because of this, there is not so much to deliberate over because now there is only one truth that needs to be expressed – simply because in any given situation either something is right, or it is wrong. If you are in doubt, you simply remain quiet and refrain from taking action, until you have gained assurance on a consciousness level.

Another problem that is experienced by many Indigos is that regardless of their age, they sometimes risk - voluntarily or involuntarily - being used as channels and/or mediums for others to push through solutions or views, by people who cannot or will not stand up and fight for themselves.

In particular, this can happen in situations where Indigo Humans, with their innate ability for sensing atmospheres or dissatisfaction, etc., may unintentionally say something about the situation to people or authorities, who are able to do something to change these conditions. The story may end well, or it may not. The fact is, however, that Indigo Humans are extremely good at drawing attention to particular problems and issues as well as making unsatisfactory conditions visible while those people affected by the conditions do not even have to take their hands out of their pockets. Often those people are not even thankful when their problems are resolved or highlighted.

Unfortunately, large groups of Indigo Children and Adolescents often have less than rewarding experiences in present society when they contribute to highlighting injustices and imbalances without even wanting to - simply because they are unable to hold back the truth, either at physical, or Spiritual level. They simply must react, and often quite intensely, so that everybody around them understands the message that something is not right or needs to be addressed, updated and/or changed in these young people's lives, and preferably much quicker than the normal speed of adults at Soul level.

Children and adolescents' revolts, however, are not always targeted at the specific problem. Often, they happen within safe boundaries where adults are present who are not necessarily their own parents. These are often adults who cannot help but notice that something is wrong, somewhere in this particular child's or adolescent's life and, who is able to deal with it on their behalf.

When young people rebel, and no adults are present, this is often perceived as a lack of respect for society and other people. It can also be viewed as a lack of parental supervision and inadequate parenting of those children and that this is often the reason for their behaviour and entirely the responsibility of the parents. It is therefore the parents' responsibility to find a positive and long-lasting solution to their children's behaviour so that it is not repeated.

Channelling that happens within spiritual circles is completely different, and more relaxed where many Soul as well as Indigo Humans voluntarily choose to channel messages from the spiritual world to Earth. Unfortunately, these days there are many people in society with tons of Crystal Energy in their auras, who have yet to be crystallized and who, during the Indigo period, have had to stay at Indigo level with their Crystal consciousness. This is simply because up until now, the Crystal Energy was incapable of getting through to the conscious sphere of Earth in its pure form – and not all of those people have positive experiences with the concept of channelling.

Many of them have, without knowing it themselves, been used as channels or mediums for countless messages that clairvoyants and trance media, etc. have brought through to their clients and listeners without knowing the overall energy picture behind the scene. The mediums believed that most of these messages had come from great beings within the spiritual world, but that in reality were channelled to them through people with great spiritual consciousness, and who were physically very much alive. Unfortunately, for those who had involuntarily been used as channels or mediums, their auras had not been crystallized and transformed, which is why they had been unable to control the use (and misuse) of their Spiritual capability.

So, it is through these crystal-clear people, who were unaware that they possessed much more Spiritual Energy than they were able to contain within their Soul and Indigo auras at the time, that so much spiritual channelling has taken place. These individuals have acted as spiritual channels and/or mediums for various media, clairvoyants and other spiritual seekers here on Earth, who – without thinking about the bigger picture and certainly without asking permission – have gleaned information from those auras, as they were themselves incapable of gathering the information from their own spiritual consciousness.

The ability to channel via other people's aura gradually disappears at Crystal level, as most people fully crystallize in their auras and bodies, becoming pure Crystal sources, and able to handle their own spiritual potential, in whichever way they find most suitable. Fully crystallized Crystal Humans then become capable of using their own inner spiritual knowledge consciously and constructively in their everyday lives, without letting other people step into their energy zone.

For those people who have yet to crystallize in their auras and bodies, there is only one thing that can be done which is to continuously draw their own Spiritual Energy back to themselves and this quickly turns out to be a lifelong task. You see, if they choose not to undergo an AuraTransformation™, which gathers their Spiritual Energy closely around their bodies, serving as a protective cape for the physical energy, they may end up spending the rest of their lives pulling back and 'cleaning up' while their environment keeps feeding off their Spiritual Energy.

Unfortunately, certain people with Indigo auras still may suffer because part of their Spiritual Energy farthest away from their bodies, is used for channelling energy by others even after their AuraTransformation™. This can happen up until their auras and bodies are fully crystallized and in that case, it would happen only in the outermost part of their aura, which of course is not okay, unless they have accepted it themselves.

It is, therefore, particularly important to try to speed up your Body Crystallization Process, even though you must be very careful in doing so. Consuming additional herbs and supplements to boost the immune system can increase the speed of the Body Crystallization. This will help to strengthen and balance your physical body and make room for the Spiritual Energy to start entering your body all the way down to cell level. In addition, weight training has a very positive effect on increasing the speed of the Body Crystallization.

In this way, you can shield the Spiritual Energy in your Crystal aura and your physical body that others wish to draw upon for channelling processes. Then, you are able to perceive other people's energy violations as physical violations, close to or within your own body. Fortunately, it is possible to address these energy breaches through a number of Balancing sessions provided by an Aura Mediator™ or via massage therapy.

Even if it sounds strange, this energy disruption can actually be massaged out of the body if you know a really good deep-tissue massage therapist, whom you trust. The massage will provide a deep physical release where it is possible to gradually get to the centre of your own energy.

There is actually only one unfortunate side effect in connection with quickly pulling back your energy, which is that you risk putting on weight during the elimination process. Unfortunately, it may take just as long to lose the weight as it does for the physical body to complete the Crystallization, i.e. several months or years. However, it is better to keep the full Spiritual Energy inside your shielded Crystal aura where it appears as an enlarged protective sphere, until the day when the Spiritual Energy has been fully integrated into your body. Or you can let all your Spiritual Energy directly into your physical body together with the energy 'straws' that some mediums use to channel energy through to themselves and others, in order to better cope with your own energies and to protect your energy balance. You may then be lucky enough that the actual medium feels inspired to suddenly cut off all contact with their channel, i.e. you, the crystallized person, as it is not always interesting to be shut inside a consciousness room or universe that is not their own.

The energies of others that have entered into your aura or body by accident will do everything they can to quickly get back out, as a physical body surrounded by a strong Crystal aura will come across as an energy prison for anything that does not rightfully belong there. In that case the penetrating energies run the risk of being fried slowly in the Spiritual Energy of the crystallized person, where the Fire element burns deeper and deeper into cell level inside the person's physical body. This is a situation that those mediums would not wish to experience at a physical level in their own lives, but which they will eventually sense on some level and at some point in their lives.

If an aura-transformed Indigo Human previously experienced channelling messages from deceased people who communicated through his or her physical body (which is preferred by deceased people as long as they are still in the Earth's energy sphere), this communication path will be shut down at the same time. In return, however, it becomes possible to communicate through the aura, which is perceived as less confrontational than when deceased people communicate through your physical body.

At a symbolic level you could say that fully crystallized humans only invite deceased people into their yard, not into their house, whereas Indigo and Soul Humans have difficulty distinguishing between house and yard.

Deceased Souls, who have used a particular channel for a long period of time, will automatically fight their way out of that individual's spiritual consciousness, if they are in the process of becoming crystallized. Also, there may be people in a Crystallizing Humans' environment, who have unknowingly channelled energy through Crystallized Humans' spiritual consciousness for many years, who will automatically wish to get away from those individuals - often without a real explanation.

Fortunately, channelling is not negatively impacted by everyone in the spiritual world, whether they are at one consciousness level or another. You see, a small exclusive group of people across the world possesses a very strong spiritual consciousness, of which they are fully aware themselves, and which they use to keep in touch with other consciousnesses, planets, galaxies, etc. outside this solar system. This contact and many of the channellings that get through via these people, however, can rarely be comprehended here on Earth at this time. Most often, the messages can be compared to visions of the future, as Leonardo da Vinci had access to in his time, approximately 400 years before it became possible to realize his visions in the physical world.

These messages are often general in nature, and since a certain form of collaboration with consciousnesses outside this solar system will not commence until 2012, when the troops have been gathered within the solar system, so to speak, those people run the risk of losing their grounding when channelling. The lack of grounding is a result of this consciousness connection with other solar systems, which cannot yet take place with balance-energy (i.e. energy with anti-poles) as a disseminating energy, but perhaps through light energy, which in its pure form is detrimental for the physical body tissue. This is described under 'Body Crystallization'.

In many ways channelling messages from alien consciousnesses outside of our solar system can be compared with contacting your government to ask for help to fix things in your own home. You may get a reply from them, but only rarely is it a tangible solution, as authorities in general know nothing about the actual human, emotional and mental conditions of your specific situation. Similarly, foreign consciousnesses outside our solar system do not always understand the physical conditions here on Earth.

Consciousness descension and ascension

When spiritual beings from foreign solar systems and universes meet in the real world here on Earth, and are then acquainted with the material world, many of them get an energetic culture shock. This can happen even if prior to their descension to Earth, they have stopped by Venus or Neptune to get tuned into earthly conditions, as these two planets represent the most spiritual high-frequency planets in our solar system.

To be clear on this point, however, I should point out that this used to be more of a problem earlier on when people were born into the earthly Soul Energy and it was possible to get directly to Earth from, for example, Neptune, which is not possible at Crystal level today.

It is one thing to experience Earth from the outside, by studying life on this planet from a distance far 'up' in the strongholds of Venus and Neptune. It is a completely different story to stand with your own feet 'down' on the physical surface of Earth and feel the physical energies everywhere around you. You must experience this yourself with grounding in the physical human body to be able to comment on the conditions here on this planet with a sense of physical realism.

However, this does not prevent many spiritual advisors around the universes, who are called upon daily by countless spiritual people here on Earth through prayer, meditation and channelling, from commenting on earthly conditions, even though the so-called spiritual advisors were never incarnated on this planet.

Unfortunately, due to the strong urge to constantly search foreign universes with their spiritual, loving and/or mental consciousness to find recognition of their spiritual truth and divine aspect deep inside themselves, many extremely spiritual people have had their Soul aura completely burned by the pure Spiritual Fire. They have therefore ended up even more sensitive and vulnerable as adults than they were when they were born.

Regretfully, this is a consciousness condition that more and more Aura Mediators™ experience with very spiritual clients when they contact them to undergo an AuraTransformation™, regardless of whether they were born with special spiritual abilities, such as clairvoyance, etc. or if they have an abstract, extremely visionary way of thinking, which is 'out of the box' compared to how life used to be viewed here on Earth.

Those people, therefore, have a completely pure Spiritual Energy and are surrounded by light where the physically dense aura ought to be, which makes them appear almost transparent in relation to their physical environment. Other spiritual people are able to pick up on their energy as they are on the exact same level of consciousness. The missing aura, however, makes it impossible for spiritual people to manifest themselves as physical beings in the material world, because earthly people are unable to perceive Spiritual Energy. Instead, they are able to relate to a visible, earthly aura, particularly if it appears as a sparkling crystal (read: *diamond*).

At consciousness level, the pure Spiritual Energy appears as a high-frequency Fire that burns its way through people's aura and consciousness as pure truth, when they are ready to look the earthly reality and the cosmic truth in the eyes.

In comparison, the Soul Energy is a constructed energy, which used to belong to the physical Earth and was much more physically dense than the Spiritual Energy. This is why the Soul Energy can be inflammable and perish. A high-frequency, balanced Crystal aura cannot perish, as it is based on a union of pure spiritual consciousness and dense Crystal Energy with a survival-oriented physical coding.

In the Crystal Energy, light is on equal terms with darkness, and Spirit is on equal terms with physicality. There is no predominance on either side, as it is the balancing of the extremes that is important. Balance is of similar importance when Crystal Humans carry out their life mission, as this is also a matter of balancing and combining the spiritual aspect with the earthly aspect.

Whether these hyper-spiritual individuals are able to cope with an earthly existence depends greatly on their fundamental consciousness energy and their knowledge of earthly matters that they acquired before arriving here. However, generally speaking, such individuals are not geared up to follow earthly rules and social guidelines. They either appear physically weak without the ability to find their way in the physical world, or there is something a bit criminal about them in an earthly sense, without them actually being criminals. This may be because they break all past norms by focusing exclusively on their own inner vision and/or inner flow without considering their environment and the way society generally works. This is particularly evident e.g. in relation to having fixed meeting times, which few spiritual beings will allow themselves to be subjected to, as they often feel that this contributes to reducing their personal creativity.

This is why very few spiritual people are suited for working in a store or a company with fixed opening hours. They would rather take a phone call whenever there are customers in the store than sit around waiting for customers to show up.

In many ways it can be difficult for practical earthy types to cooperate in projects with highly spiritual people on the team, as the latter are often much more focused on the vision and/or the group dynamics than finding a solution for the tasks at hand. They do not always get their sleeves rolled up when there are tasks to be completed, but would love to help out as advisors on mental and psychological matters for the rest of the team.

Spiritual people can therefore be a complete turn off for earthly practical people, without the spiritual people even understanding why. The individual consciousness platform for each is simply too different for either of the parties to meet in the middle. This, on the other hand, becomes an interesting challenge in the future when the Crystal Energy is fully integrated here on Earth.

Crystal Humans always weigh the balance of their spirituality and physical presence. To them, it is just as important to lend a physical hand to a project, as it is to create a good atmosphere and set positive intentions. They know that money is one way of balancing people's internal 'help account' and that we as humans cannot cope without food, drink, heat, rest and oxygen, as well as other necessities that appear at the bottom of Maslow's hierarchy of needs.

2012 will be the year when the focus will really be on achieving an overall balance between this solar system and this Earth vs. the great cosmos out there, so that we will no longer have to be bombarded by light in its pure form, as if the Earth were an uncontrollable cancer tumour that needs to be bombarded with chemo therapy. This is how it often felt from the mid 1980s up until today.

It is totally appropriate to use spiritual light to lighten dense physicality in, for example, physically oriented people's bodies and auras, as well as to lighten human ignorance, as in many places, e.g. in India where there is so much physical and human misery. However, it is definitely not appropriate for hyper-spiritual people to work with pure light as a healing modality if they already have too much light in their system. In that way they run the risk of breaking down their ability to materialize on a physical dimension and their physical power to change the world around them.

Where spiritual people voluntarily seek out spiritual experiences in their earthly lives, earthly physical people perceive that kind of experience as uncomfortable and incomprehensible. The earthy types will do anything to suppress and forget such experiences by filing them in their subconscious under the category 'inexplicable events'.

This reaction is mostly seen among people, who have lived a vast number of consecutive lives here on Earth, with the purpose of undergoing a gradual spiritual ascension by increasing their human consciousness through the wisdom they acquire on this planet.

Earthy people, who feel the Spirit breathe down their neck, have always viewed this as a sign that death was just around the corner, but in the Crystal Time, this has an entirely different meaning. Instead, it indicates an extraordinary expansion of consciousness while still being alive and in your right mind as a human.

In the Indigo and Crystal Energies, respectively, but not in the Soul Energy, it is possible from a physical and consciousness perspective to live several lifetimes during the same life. At least that is how the individual perceives it.

You see, each dimension that we humans go through in connection with our consciousness development represents a phase of life in itself. Each such dimension and phase of life can be integrated either over several months or years, during which time you may be very close to some people that you might never see again in this physical life. Or perhaps you will meet them in a later dimension or consciousness phase, when each party has integrated new energies, with which they can enrich themselves and each other. This is exactly the same as when you meet people in your current life that you know from several lifetimes ago on a Soul level.

Case

Søren Peter Jensen, a 39 year-old man from Denmark, usually describes his life as being as if he were "dumped on Earth where others have already read the first two chapters of the book. There is no chance of catching up on the reading. No bookstore and no library has the book, because it is read while you live".

For everyone else, knowing the content of those first two chapters is a matter of course, and nobody can or will tell Søren what it says in those two chapters of the 'Manual for life here on Earth'. They don't even understand the necessity of explaining it to him.

"I was born in 1969 into what must be described as a 'working family'. I am the youngest of four children. My mother was a stay-at-home mum until I was eight years old. I was very close to my mother, whereas my memories of my father paint a picture of a very absent person. He was the authority figure and what I remember most clearly from my relationship with him was fear of scolding, supervision and being corrected. I was a different child, very reserved. I lived very much in my own little fantasy world. I was good at making up games for myself and I played with dolls and knitted, not exactly your typical interests for a 'normal' boy. If I was placed together with other children, I still played alone. I have memories throughout my childhood of constantly longing to be allowed to play along, to be part of what I saw others do, and experience some of what I read about in the stacks of books I dragged home from the library each week - friendships, games and later on parties. I didn't understand what made me different. Each time I tried, I failed. I was awkward in my appearance. I hated physical education where my total lack of physical presence was extremely obvious. I was always the last one to be picked whenever we had to form teams. I was an easy target for bullying, as I was completely unprotected. Anything that was said went straight inside of me. No filter. At home no one understood. It was either "poor me" or "it was probably my own fault – what a wimp I was!" The teachers didn't do anything – the worst ones even took part in the bullying.

Somehow I didn't care. In a way, I thought that what the others did and said was stupid. Already back then, I had a sense of perspective and was able to see through contexts that only a few others could. I have often been told that I was wilful and cross. I withdrew into my own, safe fantasy world. Still, what I remember most of all is the loneliness and the longing to be part of everything.

As a teenager I didn't belong to any cliques and didn't go to any parties. Instead, I found my way to the Whitsun Church. For the first time, I found something here that reminded me of a community that I could be part of, and a form of acceptance. I had always been fascinated by the stories of the Bible. As a child I sang in a church choir. I remember that, already back then, I had some very intense experiences during the services; experiences of being at home where I belonged. It was as if what was written in the Bible, in the psalms and in what the minister said, were truths that I knew already. It therefore felt natural to me to enter into a Christian community. This, however, had severe consequences. My father was very much against it, which created even more tension at home. In addition, I had just discovered that I was gay, and my inner conflict was absolute. After two years I had to realize that these two things could not be reconciled, and I left the church.

When I was 21 years old I moved to Copenhagen. I had a hard time handling the jobs I had, especially the social aspect. I managed by playing the clown and imitating what I saw. Again, I was left with a feeling of not belonging, not being part of anything.

I became an active member of the National Association for Gays and Lesbians (LBL) and suddenly a new door opened up for me. I quickly read the codes for the traditional gay person and played the part to a tee. I was able to put to good use my keen perspective in many situations within the organization. In fact, I started to feel that people appreciated me, even looked up to me. Once in a while, however, I was caught. Perhaps

I overplayed my role and stepped on people's toes. Back then I hadn't heard of words like 'grounding', but I didn't own it. I floated through life and often didn't understand the trifling problems that people in my circles were carrying around. My own problems were big and existential. It was all about learning how to live, about being allowed to be here on Earth, and about being seen and valued.

I had trouble finding an identity, a standpoint. When the volunteer work for LBL began to fade, I needed something new to hold onto. I found it in the fairytale world and I started to collect dolls and Disney cartoons. Again, I had a huge sense of 'recognition' - somewhat like the story of the Bible, the minister's words and the psalms. There was a truth to the fairytales and the dolls that I recognized - something safe, loving and aesthetically beautiful. In fact, I sometimes got physically ill from watching movies. Horror movies, violent movies and such, triggered some severe reactions in me.

Looking back today, I know that I went deep inside everything I experienced. The fact that there was no filter enabled me to go deep inside and feel the essence of everything I met. This applied to what I read, my dolls, and other people. In a sense it was exciting because sometimes the experience was beautiful and detailed. The only problem was that I couldn't feel myself at the same time. I got lost in everything without being in touch with my inner self. This became a problem for my studies. I understood everything, right down to the detail. I was able to acquaint myself with everything I read and see the dilemmas from above, but I was unable to relate to the dilemmas, let alone discuss them with my fellow students, because I was swimming around inside of them. This way of navigating through life became a serious problem in my relationships with others. You see, I used my ability to enter into other people, feel their emotions and then reasoned how to act. When having an argument, this method was very inappropriate. Not only did I completely overstep the other person's boundaries, once I was in there – rather than being in myself - I became extremely vulnerable to attacks and unable to defend myself. Naturally this meant that my own boundaries were in great danger of being overstepped as well.

About five years ago I was at a turning point in my life. I had been in a relationship with a guy for six months, who was physically abusive and an alcoholic. When I got out of the relationship in July 2004, I had a severe reaction. I became a complete zombie and totally disappeared from my body. I had some powerful spiritual experiences and hallucinations, e.g. one night I woke up with the feeling that hundreds of small blisters were growing on my legs. It became increasingly difficult to function in my job, which I had to quit in the end. I was about to fall apart completely. I saw myself as floating. At the same time I began hypnotherapy. This helped my immediate condition somewhat, but it didn't make a big difference. In hindsight I know that I was used to 'going outside of my body' whenever something became too much. In a sense, the hypnotherapy only prolonged this defence mechanism.

I then started body therapy with healing massages and dialogues. I became very confused by using two different forms of therapy at the same time and therefore stopped the hypnotherapy. The massage was very provocative for me. It was overwhelming to be forced into my body, but slowly, things began to improve. After taking long-term sickness leave, on the advice of a clairvoyant, I isolated myself a lot. I continued to see the body therapist, but the progress was very slow. After a while I made some changes. I moved into a new apartment and slowly began to see other people through courses, workshops, etc. At the beginning of 2007 I stumbled upon a website about Crystal Children (and Adults) and immediately thought, "This is about me". Everything just fit - the things that were said about being reserved, the need to withdraw, a great sense of vulnerability and great knowledge and insight, but with no opportunity or strength to succeed, resonated with me.

I left it for a while – let it grow inside of me. I was still working on myself with the body therapist. My body consciousness was still improving and I was gradually able to be present in my body, in small doses at a time. Slowly but surely, I also became better at putting my foot down. I started a course and some job training in order to re-enter the workforce. I sensed that I still 'disappeared' quite often when I was with others - like being in a fog – or walking around above others. I was able to follow everything that went on, but not be part of it myself. That is how I experienced it.

In October 2007 I went to see a clairvoyant again. I was no longer receiving sickness benefit and my livelihood was faltering. She told me to start helping other people with body treatments. My approach was to be a massage therapist and I would be receiving funding towards the training. It was liberating to be told so specifically and I immediately began to put into action what she had recommended.

In December 2007 I read about AuraTransformation™ for the first time. I had found the program for the health fair in Hillerød, Denmark, and that is where I ran across the concept of Crystal Children once again. There were going to be a couple of lectures on the topic. Again I felt very drawn to the topic and wanted to go there to hear more. The fair took place at the beginning of January 2008. When I entered the room where the lecture was about to be given, I had a very strong sense of coming home - but in a different and more present way than with the psalms, the dolls and the cartoons. I felt as if a large protective Crystal pyramid was lowered onto me. During a round of talks when the participants spoke about their interest in the topic, I said that I suspected that I was a Crystal Adult. The speaker, who saw that I was carrying a lot of the Crystal Energy, immediately confirmed my suspicion. I then knew for sure that I needed an AuraTransformation™.

I was transformed early February 2008. It felt like a completely natural part of the development I had undergone. My development really took off after the transformation. At the same fair, I met a Body SDS (Self Development System) therapist and received a trial treatment. Body SDS is a relatively new form of body treatment. It is a Danish invention that works with the whole person. It is a very physical treatment that includes pulsing massage, deep pressure and joint release. Since then I have received treatments every three weeks or so, which has had a great impact.

I am starting to experience other people and the environment around me as something that is separate from me. When I watch a movie today that I saw five years ago, the experience is completely different. I don't feel the emotions of the movie as severely as before, and it is easier for me to understand the plot. I have a clear sense of 'falling into place'. I no longer need to 'go outside of my body' as often. I have had many problems with indigestion throughout the entire process, and I am currently working hard at getting my digestive tract under control.

I have worked a lot on my diet over the past two years. It was something that I had, quite naturally, been wanting for approximately one year prior to my transformation. At the beginning, I was a vegetarian for about six months, but I then started to eat poultry and fish as well. I personally believe that this was part of a cleansing that my body needed in order to prepare for the transformation. I am now much better at sensing what is good for me. I don't have the same constant need to ask other people's advice and approval. If I sense that I am about to drift into the people that I am with, I practice withdrawing and sensing myself – this is a process that I am getting better at all the time. I am well into my training as a massage therapist. My funding has been approved, although it took a long time and put my self-confidence and patience to the test. I am developing my treatment methods while I work. I am using what I learn in school, combined with my own intuition and experience.

I have a strong feeling that I am 'from above', as if I have a total consciousness that needs a framework and grounding to be able to succeed. Actually, I have always known that my development process would happen from above and down – from outside in. It always confused me that other people worked on themselves in a different way than I. Whenever I need an answer, I often get it during body treatments, e.g. Body SDS. In addition, I feel that I am part of our Lord's energy and that I have a certain role to play in connection with that".

When Soul Humans die

I have heard many spiritually awake people consider what will happen to Soul Humans when they die and are unable to return to Earth with the same level of consciousness they had before they died.

To me, it makes absolutely no difference, whether Soul Humans need to go behind Earth's veil of consciousness in order to move to a higher vibration when they have a physical death, or whether this happens while they are alive through either an AuraTransformation™ or some other method of consciousness-expansion.

The determining factor must be, whether those individuals feel they are able to make life changes and make a consciousness shift while they are still alive; or whether it seems more manageable for them to allow this shift to happen, once they leave their physical body.

Factors, such as age or personal stubbornness can be decisive in a person's willingness to change their level of consciousness, which at best can pro-long their physical life by a few years. For instance not many older people see any advantage in changing their daily diet of roast pork, sausages and meatballs with gravy and potatoes to a basic diet rich in fibre with a focus on fruit and vegetables.

Besides, many people find it difficult to relate to a life without their daily cigarettes and a drink or two, which is often used to help take the edge off life and provide a sense of purpose. They would rather 'live life' and die sooner, if that is the consequence of their lifestyle choice.

In the Indigo Energy it is difficult for the physical body to absorb large amounts of drugs and alcohol, without the body entering into an acute state in order to purge the system of this sedative state as quickly as possible. In the Crystal Energy it is pretty much impossible for the body to relate to, say tobacco and alcohol for example, unless the alcohol has some positive nutritional value, such as in certain kinds of red wine and herbal tincture.

Crystal Humans, however, have no problem consuming alcohol to enjoy the taste, although only in small amounts, which is why we must assume that there will be a substantial decline in the sale of tobacco, alcohol and drugs in the future.

If Soul Humans choose to die, rather than have a consciousness upgrade while they are alive, many of them will undergo a spiritual transformation of their energy in connection with their own physical death, which leads them directly to the Spiritual level. You see, these days all Soul Energy is disappearing from the aura when a person dies, which is why it is no longer possible to be born with Soul Energy here on Earth.

It is no longer possible to incarnate with Soul Energy on any other planet in the solar system, either, unless you look in the direction of the Moon, which on a consciousness level has belonged to a different solar system since the year 2000, even though physically, it is still in this solar system.

The Soul Energy, which originates from the Moon, is a physically dense state of consciousness that is either totally or partially physically visible to very few people. In most other places in the great Universe, you move around as a Spiritual Energy in various heavy or light energy forms.

The Soul Energy represents a physical template, in which the Spirit lived in the Old Time Energy. This was to enable spiritual beings of varying levels of consciousness, from within and outside this solar system, to relate to each other by immediately recognizing each other's energy.

It therefore became easier for humans here on Earth to develop

certain human and consciousness qualities for the benefit of themselves and the collective, even though originally their respective fundamental energies were very different.

It used to be that if the Soul Energy did not let go of the deceased person's body right away, the Soul would wander about in the Earth's heavy layer of energy like a ghost, which has been much more common in some parts of the world than others. This can still occur today, if the deceased Soul either has a low degree of energy or a high degree of physicality while feeling a great sense of belonging to the old Soul-controlled Earth. This is why you may at times experience extremely heavy and physically dense energies in some areas, e.g. where the population and/or individuals stubbornly fight to remain in touch with the past or their deceased loved ones. In such areas, the population is often as dense in the backing of the Earth's consciousness just behind the veil as it is at the visible physical level.

If deceased Souls are predestined to continue on as Soul Humans in their next lives, this will require them to follow the Moon's energy into a different solar system. Alternatively, all deceased Souls will have to have their energy transformed to pure Spiritual Energy, once they get out of the Earth's heavy sphere.

If previous Souls are meant to return to Earth to take on a future life mission here, they are going to have their energy upgraded to pure Spiritual Energy in order to be born as today's Crystal Children. However, this will not happen until after their respective energies have been cleansed and their consciousness level updated on a physical planet within or outside the solar system or somewhere in the cosmic spheres.

If their energies are unable to fit into the earthly Crystal format, the solution may be to meld together several equal spiritual consciousnesses at a consciousness level, so that together they will match the present-day aura structure of the Earth. In this way, little five-year-old Lisa may turn out to be extraordinarily similar to both her deceased grandmother as well as her deceased aunt - because to them, she is just their little Lisa.

When spiritual people die, their Spiritual Energy slowly and quietly releases their physical body. This can happen over a short or a long period of time during which all parties, including the person themselves, are fully aware that the time is approaching for the Spirit to say its final goodbye to the physical body. This is just as it happened among Native Americans back in time. The spirit, however, may also choose to leave the body quickly as the person themselves regulates the spiritual-physical vibration of the physical body.

In no way does the Spirit feel tied to the body. The spiritual-physical fusion is exclusively due to the fact that the two forces must work together in the best possible way during the Crystal Period. The Spirit is therefore not the body, but through fusion with the body, the body is enabled to vibrate at the same frequencies as the Spiritual Energy, only in a more physical way. The Spirit therefore has no problem getting out of its physical shell when the day comes to say goodbye to Earth and the physical environment.

If middle aged and particularly older people have a body structure that has difficulty adapting from Soul frequencies to Crystal frequencies because of a lack of Crystal potential, their physical bodies will quite naturally and gradually break down while the Earth moves farther and farther into its Crystal phase. There was always a period in their lives here on Earth, for elderly and old people, that was more 'their time' than others – a time when they particularly thrived. Only rarely does that period occur towards the end of their lives, as they should then be able to live even longer and continue their physical lives into the next era.

The condition of the physical body is therefore a deciding factor for determining whether a person's energy can be transformed into higher frequencies or not while you are physically alive.

This and that on New Time Energy and what it takes to get there

Her følger en række vigtige spørgsmål og svar i relation til Ny Tids energi, som ikke absolut har noget med hinanden at gøre, men som helt sikkert er interessante at vide for den videnshungrende læser:

Important prerequisites for undergoing an AuraTransformation™

All people carry the truth within them. It is only a question of how deeply they want to dig in order to find the answers. Many people do not always want real answers to their questions. They would rather have their many wishes fulfilled, which unfortunately do not always represent the inner truth for them.

This is a fact that is extremely important to keep in mind when discussing whether or not an individual feels ready to undergo an AuraTransformation™: how close do they really wish to get to themselves and their inner truth?

There is a great degree of truth connected with undergoing an AuraTransformation™ as your energies move into much higher frequencies than ever before and once they do that, everything seems deeper and more intense than before, which cannot be explained in words. The zest for life and the joy in many things becomes deeper as does the resentment towards the many bad things that are happening around the world and within your immediate environment as they violate your inner truth and balance.

It is a prerequisite for undergoing an AuraTransformation™ to feel ready to relate to the world around you in a pragmatic and realistic way, in which you see things as they really are and not as you want them to be.

You see, when reality knocks in the New Time, you cannot just quickly pull the illusionary veil of the past in front of the door and keep focused on a dream-like scenario in front of you. On the other hand, reality may bring about new and much greater opportunities than we ever imagined in our wildest dreams.

No matter what, it is important to be thoroughly informed about the impact of an AuraTransformation™ prior to undergoing one. If you do not want any change in your life, you should completely refrain from being aura transformed and instead stick to the life you know so well and feel safe and comfortable with.

When is it unsuitable to undergo an AuraTransformation™?

It is not suitable for a person to have his or her aura transformed if the individual is old - particularly old in spirit.

If a person is mentally ill or mentally unstable and/or dependent on strong medication or alcohol, or if a person takes hallucinogenic drugs, including smoking marijuana, etc., the Aura Mediator™ will refuse to aura transform the individual in 99.9% of the cases for the person's own sake.

There must be very mitigating circumstances in order for the Aura Mediator™ to deviate from the rule of not aura transforming clients who are on strong medication and/or happy pills. If the individual is an alcoholic and/or drug abuser, the Aura Mediator™ will consistently refuse to aura transform the person.

The outcome of the AuraTransformation™ for people who smoke marijuana can be difficult to predict exactly. This is because the effect of marijuana usually remains in the individual's body and consciousness for a long time after consumption and has a tremendously distorting effect on the person's ability to comprehend clearly, even if the individual does not perceive the situation as such. This is why an AuraTransformation™ is not recommended if you are a frequent user of marijuana; naturally it is a different story if you have only smoked marijuana once or twice.

If a spiritually focused person wishes to undergo an AuraTransformation™ as one of many consciousness-expanding spiritual experiences on his or her journey in search of their inner truth, an AuraTransformation™ is usually turned down by the Aura Mediator™ because an AuraTransformation™ cannot be reversed if a person regrets his or her decision at a later point. You see, once the aura has been transformed into an Indigo or Crystal aura, there is no way for your personal consciousness to return to Soul Land, other than to visit old Soul friends on their consciousness home ground, which at that point will no longer be the home ground of the aura-transformed individual.

It is all a question of personal evaluation in each situation though, as there are usually exceptions to the rules. The essence of this section of the book, however, is that an AuraTransformation™ should not be taken lightly and that it requires great personal responsibility to become aura transformed. This is the reason why anyone who wishes to undergo an AuraTransformation™ is asked to read carefully about the consequences of their consciousness choice in one or more of my previous books on this subject, before they are allowed in the Aura Mediator's chair to be aura transformed.

In relation to those people around the world who still have a lot of karma to phase out at Soul level, the Aura Mediator™ does not even need to consider whether or not those individuals are ready to undergo an AuraTransformation™: those people would never come up with the idea of an AuraTransformation™ as this is not part of their destiny.

Can young, pregnant women have their energies upgraded through the foetus?

There are different determining factors for humans with Indigo auras than for humans with *transitional energy*, who have a mix of Soul and Indigo auras.

For instance, young women with transitional energy will not automatically become fully transformed during their pregnancy so that they end up with a pure Indigo aura even though they are carrying a young child with Crystal Energy in their uterus.

If their Indigo aura is almost complete, in that they only have little Soul Energy left in the aura structure, they may be lucky enough that they, through the energy influx from their unborn child, become adjusted and/ or fully transformed during the pregnancy. However, if they have a lot of Soul Energy in their aura, the transformation cannot happen, as the foetus does not have the same physical force of manifestation as a newborn child as it is still linked to the mother's energy and considered a part of her consciousness. And, as previously mentioned, no one can perform their own AuraTransformation™.

Expectant mothers with Indigo auras, on the other hand, can start to increase the speed of or complete their Crystallization Process during the pregnancy, and so obtain a pure Crystal aura and fully crystallize their bodies at the same time. There are generally no problems connected with performing an AuraTransformation™ on pregnant women, as long as they feel ready for it. Their energy will thus better match that of the foetus.

If the parents are not aura transformed, what about the children?

For a fully body crystallized person, an AuraTransformation™ will, in many ways, seem like the icing on the cake regarding what it means to be a totally balanced human being. However, not all adults have such positive thoughts about having their auras transformed, regardless if they are body crystallized or not.

Seen from the outside, this may not interest you at all if this is about adults who only need to take care of themselves and each other. However, as soon as there are children involved in the lives of adults who are at a consciousness standstill, someone has to care, because there is a real risk of these children being slowed down in their own consciousness development because of their parents' choice of life from a consciousness perspective.

Children who are born with a transitional aura between Soul and Indigo Energy will rarely be stimulated by their non-transformed parents into having their aura adjusted to either pure Indigo or pure Crystal Energy. However, they can naturally start to body crystallize just like everybody else. Once they are adults themselves, we can only hope that they will choose to have their auras fully transformed. And who knows – perhaps there is a higher meaning in the delay of their consciousness upgrade?

All Indigo Children are born with a fundamental balance, but they are often out of balance because of their environment. The children, however, will spontaneously find their balance in relation to themselves and their environment as years go by and the Crystal Energy gains increased acceptance around the world.

In no way are Indigo Children dependent of their parents' consciousness standpoint in life, but they will naturally react to any imbalances in the home and in their daily environment, as long as they are subject to that framework.

As soon as Indigo Children are removed from various negative impacts in their daily lives, they no longer react to imbalances that are not a direct part of their new experience.

It is therefore advantageous to move around in the New Time Energy without bringing along your baggage, especially if the moves aim at changing the imbalances in the children's lives in a more positive direction. The children's reactions will likewise be changed in a more positive direction.

Crystal Children cannot help but stimulate their non-transformed parents to take a more positive direction thereby creating some sort of a consciousness awakening within their parents,

for the benefit of the children and the parents themselves. However, it will mainly be the parents' bodies that respond to the children's Crystal Energy, if it is not possible to also transform their auras. We will therefore see many non-transformed parents of Crystal Children starting to become more conscious about looking after their physical bodies through physical exercise and a change of diet, etc.

Crystal Children are therefore not running the risk of suffering at home or in institutions as they will make sure to get things the way they instinctively and intuitively know they ought to be.

We are therefore going to see quite a few non-transformed adults in the future who, without thinking about it, follow the lines that their children and the surrounding society lay out for them. These adults, however, must pull their personal plug from time to time, in order to recharge by themselves or both together, if they are in a relationship. These people will not contribute anything extraordinary to this world, but will continue to learn from life instead, as it is done at Soul level. The environment, however, will have no doubt, whether those people are at Soul level or Indigo or Crystal level, as their human capacity and interest in the outside world will reflect their respective level of energy.

If the non-transformed adults are lucky enough to body crystallize based on a healthy diet and regular exercise as well as communing with nature, they will be much better off from a consciousness perspective than if they were not crystallized at all. This is because they will at least then expose their life mission down at cell level in their physical bodies and have an inner truth to follow here in life, which is much better than were they to have no visible truth to live by.

It is worth keeping in mind though, that the chances of body crystallizing, without having first undergone an Aura Crystallization/AuraTransformation™, are not equally good in all parts of the world. The Japanese, for example, will generally have a much better chance of Body Crystallization despite their high daily pace in the big cities than say Americans. This is because the Japanese have a very healthy and pure food culture with a focus on foods, such as tofu, fish and vegetables that nourish the physical body, whereas many Americans tend to eat fast food and big steaks.

It should also be pointed out that not everybody is geared to learn through their karma at Soul level first, in order to then go into the world at Spiritual level to teach others the things they have learned as part of their life mission/Dharma. Perhaps these individuals have grown too old to adapt their lives to the modern Crystal lifestyle, or they did not bring their full, original, spiritual pool this time around, which is why they are much better equipped to undergo the upgrade to Spiritual Energy on the other side of the veil between Earth and the surrounding solar system. It should not be painful to move beyond your existing consciousness boundaries, but rather it should be personally liberating.

Do you need repeated Balancing sessions after your AuraTransformation™?

Balancing sessions with the help of an Aura Mediator™ mostly influence your personal balance and your personal well-being which is why several Balancing sessions are rarely needed after an AuraTransformation™ and in certain cases no subsequent balancing is needed at all.

Balancing to keep up your energy level once the balance has occurred is simply a waste of time and money as a balanced mind is always able to balance itself.

Unless the balancing is part of the aura and the Body Crystallization, the latter of which may stretch over several years, there is no need for ongoing Balancing sessions.

However, you should never let Balancing sessions lull you into a false sense of security, which might keep you from responding to your energetic impulses in the time up until the 'last' Balancing session has taken place.

Only if you have many blockages in your body and/or undesirable, negative body memories do you need repeated Balancing sessions after your AuraTransformation™. In this case, it should preferably be a body balancing, through which old undesirable coding in the body is overwritten right down to cell level in order for the New Time Crystal Balancing Energy to occur. This may be in the form of massage, Body SDS, cupping and such.

During the Crystallization Phase, continuous energy treatments and Balancing sessions will mainly act as a kick-start for people, who are really tormented by their energy, body and/or mind in their search for physical and personal balance. As soon as New Time Humans are balanced in their bodies and minds, and therefore in their entire consciousness, energy as a separate concept, will take up less and less room in their consciousness, as the energy will develop into a lifestyle, rather than just being an interest.

Crystal Humans are very active and holistic people who want to change the world at a visible level, and they also wish to make anything that can be made visible in the consciousness universe visible to people in the earthly sphere. By no means do they wish to linger in the energy receiving massages all the time, while the world passes by outside the window. They want to get out there and take part in life themselves.

Can two or more chakras be merged prior to the AuraTransformation™?

At some point, one of our trained Aura Mediators wrote to me that, before she underwent her AuraTransformation™ and unknowingly, with regards to her energy, had worked at merging her chakras at Soul level as her consciousness had an inner knowledge that that was how things were supposed to be. I do not believe, however, that this is possible without messing up the system, as merging of people's chakras belongs at Indigo and Crystal level, respectively.

Undeniably, there is a big difference between having a completely open house (i.e. the body), where the rooms (a.k.a. the chakras) and the energies gradually flow into each other in a balanced way, to consciously turn two rooms into one (e.g. kitchen and washroom), as if it were the same thing. The general chakra fusion does not work in such a way that the ingredients can just be thrown into the pot, without focusing on the combination of flavours because then we risk, figuratively speaking, mixing together faeces with our food, or getting stinky feet in our face.

Pardon the symbolism, but it helps get the message through about not mixing things that can easily find a balance on their own. But, in this case, the fusion had happened subconsciously back at Soul level, and it was thus completely unintentional.

AuraTransformation™ vs. Personal Reconnection

In principle, Eric Pearl's 'Personal Reconnection' and AuraTransformation™ consist of identical spiritual processes.
With a Personal Reconnection, however, the client remains at Soul level in the old aura structure with his or her personal energy and body energy, whereas an AuraTransformation™ helps the client out of the Soul Energy and onto the Spiritual level with a direct connection to the divine source through the body instead.

Personal Reconnection is for spiritual searchers, who wish to stay on safe ground in their existing energies, whereas an AuraTransformation™ is for people, who wish to act out their spirituality in their physical life.

AuraTransformation™ vs. Deeksha

Several people have asked me to touch on that topic in this book. Personally, I would have preferred to avoid the subject, as I risk coming across as someone who completely disassociates from Deeksha, which is not the case. My personal opinion on Deeksha is that lots of people can benefit from the energy in that part of the world where the energy impulse originates, i.e. India, where the population has a much more physically dense body and aura structure than the majority of people in the far North.

Deeksha can be an advantage in helping people get their aura and body energies going and loosen up old locked energy patterns and ties, thereby making it easier for these individuals to let go of the system. Once the blockages have been released, the Deeksha energy is far from having a balancing effect on the aura and the body, though, as the energy ends up constantly burning without any personal control.

In brief, the Deeksha energy represents pure Sun energy, which many physically oriented people across the world can benefit from integrating, so that they can begin to burn through with their Spiritual Energy in the physical world. You could call the Deeksha energy a stepping-stone or a first step towards Spiritual Energy.

The Venus energy is represented through the balancing energy, which has many different, balanced frequencies, mainly at the high-frequency end of the scale.

The Deeksha energy is not balanced in a high-frequency way when compared to the high-frequency Venus Crystal Energy of the New Time. The Deeksha energy then appears as pure sunshine instead, which may blind people's sense of direction and disrupt their physical balance.

Many people are fascinated by the Sun energy, but as we know from the physical sun, the energy tends to burn far too severely in the physical world resulting in actual physical burns, if you are not careful. This particularly tends to happen if Crystal Humans choose to work with pure Deeksha energy without a main focus on the balancing energy. The Deeksha energy can work as a good supplement for the New Time balancing energy if the energy is used to break down old physical density in people's minds and bodies.

Physically oriented people with dark skin can benefit from being in the Sun energy, as we see it on the Earth's Southern hemisphere, whereas high-frequency balance-oriented people are often burned by the energy because the Sun-inspired Deeksha energy disrupts their spiritual-physical and physical-personal balance – and often their mental balance as well.

Below is a short story to illustrate how the Sun energy, in a completely different context, can easily become too much for others at consciousness level, which may have fatal consequences in those people's physical lives:

"Many years ago I had a girlfriend who had a very strong Sun energy. When she met her Moon husband, who was much more introverted and moody than her and, who acted through his very own inner balance, they were simply unable to sleep in the same room. The problem was that he got completely burned in her energy presence and interestingly enough, shortly thereafter he began to drink more alcohol than usual - perhaps to douse the energy fire. You see, she sensed how his energy was different from hers, which is why she at consciousness level stayed half awake all night in order to burn her way through to his energy system, and therefore neither one of them got the physical sleep they needed."

So, you must be careful not to integrate too much light in this earthly universe without keeping your focus on the balance. Because it destroys the body structure and the Earth's physically dense energy structure right down to cell level, if the light energy is not balanced with the physical energy.

Schizophrenia explained from an energy point of view

Schizophrenia is generally caused by an individual having several cons-ciousness standpoints and/or affiliations, rather than just one at a time, as most earthly humans have. Many schizophrenics often have a very strong consciousness affiliation with the planet that they originate from in the solar system, which is why they relate all daily events to the conditions on their home planet. Because of their lack of consciousness integration in the earthly universe, they are either fully or partially incapable of relating to everyday life in an earthly context.

Unfortunately, those people are rarely fully conscious about the fragmentation of their consciousness and the subsequent personal division.

From an energy perspective, the concept of schizophrenia can be explained as a person being bilingual or multilingual but who, unfortunately, does not know how to keep each language apart when they want to express themselves to others. The individual thus mixes together several energy terms that are not always possible to translate into the human language and are not easy to understand. This makes the particular person appear uncollected in his or her physical association with others in their everyday lives.

Different types of energies that focus on dark energy and love energy

Resistance that is not an integral part of humans' consciousness development or maturing can always be traced back to the dark energy meaning the 'anti-Christ', 'anti-God' and Satanism or another kind of negative energy, and the very dense and obdurate physical and mental feminine energy in humans, who prefer standstill and familiar conditions and topics, rather than life and masculine activity. The anti-force is also called anti-Crystal, depending in which of the energy frequencies it is expressed.

Sometimes, the dark energy tries to curb your spiritual development by creating inconvenient resistance towards you in your physical everyday life, so that you no longer have the energy to look forward and creatively regarding your own personal development and your life in general. When this happens, you should infuse the resistance with pure love, which is the essence of both Spiritual and Physical Energy, i.e. balancing energy, because then the dark energy cannot harm you.

Light energy corresponds to the frequency where the pure spiritual impulse hits matter for the first time, i.e. the world of form, and creates a physically creative impulse and/or consciousness awakening as a thought, movement or similar. This is not the same as pure love, which is an ultimately balanced, all-embracing, inclusive and fully accepting energy that contains no opposites and therefore cannot create or respond to resistance.

On the other hand it can transform everything into divine energy, regardless of its original form. This can be seen, for example, when people pray for others out of pure love for their fellow human beings because they want to help whole-heartedly.

Unfortunately, many light workers perceive the healing energy that they work with as pure love energy, although it is really light energy they use for healing. If they work with pure love energy instead, it would be more appropriate to call themselves love or balance mediators, rather than light workers.

Pure love is thus an energy, which the dark energy and the dense, mental physicality are unable to relate to, much in the same disassociating way as it does to the Spiritual Energy where it resents the strong light. Balanced, love-oriented people do not fall apart inside if the outside world is in chaos. Neither do they fall apart on the outside if their inner world is in temporary chaos. These people understand better than anyone how to keep balance in all circumstances of life and how to keep the love for themselves and others, no matter if physical-spiritual balance is present in their lives or not.

Always look at the sexual energy and the pure love energy that correspond to the masculine and the feminine energy, as your allies at a Spiritual as well as on an earthly level. You see, the aim is to connect these two energies at the earthly level, the way they are connected at the Spiritual level, which has not previously been possible in the low-frequency earthly energies. This is because, contrary to common belief, the Earth's fundamental energy is guided by a strong, dense, all-embracing, feminine love energy that, like a second Mother Earth, embraces the vigorous and pulsing masculine core, which it is our objective to reach. This is why many people subconsciously try to connect with the inner force of the Earth – the masculine energy – often through sexual energy, but do not get far enough into their own pure earthly love consciousness, allowing them to get through to the pure, unconditional, masculine sexual impulse inside the core. Regrettably, somewhere on the way there, they connect with the dark energy of the mental earthly layer instead.

The thing is, the dark energy is embedded in these dense, physically mental and feminine energy layers that originally consisted of pure love energy and which surrounds the masculine, vigorous and pulsing core inside the Earth. These energy layers emerged as a result of the multiple mental vibrations that humans have sent into the Earth's energy sphere throughout time, hoping to materialize their wishes at the physical level. The dark energy thus emerged as a 'hodgepodge' of everyone's diverse and completely different spiritual and physical thoughts, wants, manifestations, visualizations, mantras, etc. that have connected with the feminine part of the Earth's magnetic field. These are the thoughts and mental manifestations that have helped create the reality and the mentality here on Earth throughout time in a predominantly negative and locked condition. When too many different forces try to get their share of the cake at the same time, without considering anyone's needs but their own, the energy blocks and creates this locked condition, i.e. physical and spiritual standstill as well as a general obduracy, which is how the anti-force appears under earthly and spiritual auspices.

The dark energy can thus be briefly described as the sum of all people's completely different thoughts, focusing entirely on their own individual needs, leaving out the needs of others. The Crystal Energy, on the contrary, focuses on the individual as well as of others at the same time, which is why the anti-force slowly, but surely, will be forced out as years go by, and the Crystal Energy gains ground in society. This is because the Crystal Energy is capable of accommodating many different facets of life and humanity without condemnation and thus carries the balancing aspect of love.

The view of energy vs. the view of humanity

As the Crystal Energy gradually spreads under the earthly auspices, there will be more focus on people's varying perspective of reality, based on their different cultural backgrounds, personal influence, etc. You see, very different views on the same things, people and life circumstances, etc. tend to part the waters between people, and often the disagreement solely originates in the view of the energy, rather than the view of humanity.

If all children were born without predetermining energy influence, spiritual or physical, from their point of origin, as well as from those energies they stayed within prior to their earthly incarnation, the world would undeniably look very different and undifferentiated. This is because all children would then start out with the same energy perspective, making their view of energy identical. The view of energy would then be the foundation for a more uniform view of humanity, where all human disagreement would be redundant, which would happen despite people's different physical genetics and position of influence here in life, etc.

The Crystal Energy places a lot of emphasis on the correlation between the view of energy and the view of humanity, so that these two ways of viewing the world do not differentiate substantially, as can happen in many places today. Not everybody functions with the same kind of balance in life, where the inner balance is one balance that often relates to the view of energy with a focus on life conditions, which each individual knows from his or her home planet.

The outer balance, on the other hand, is a different balance that often relates to the view of humanity and that can be defined in many different ways, depending on the individual's personality, lifestyle, residence and childhood, etc.

It is much easier for two people to create balance between their different views of humanity and external conditions in life than if they have different views of energy and therefore different fundamental energies at an inner level. However, it is most important to have balance between the view of energy and the view of humanity in each individual, which is the prerequisite for feeling whole as a human, independently of other people's individual balance. For once the inner and outer balances are in place within each individual, he or she can begin to create balance elsewhere in their lives, in relation to other individuals, that he or she needs in order to create a deeper, overall balance in their lives.

These are the essential points of 'Project Crystallization', which, by combining the Crystal Individual with the Crystal wholeness, results in the Crystal Human.

Life with Crystal Energy

When people are fully crystallized in their aura and body, their aura and personal 'Crystal' (diamond) fully closes around them, so that, with respect to their energy, they appear as Crystal Individuals with full access to their own source. All Crystal Individuals are their own divine sources that have God's impulse encapsulated in their own body right down to cell level.

Therefore, they no longer really need to ask other people for advice about conditions concerning themselves, as they already know all the answers. All they need to do is search within themselves, i.e. in their mind and body, to feel the effect of the reality they are in at a given time, and they will instinctively and intuitively know what to do in a specific situation.

Pure Crystal Individuals, who are born from 2009 and on, and pure Crystal Humans, who are born from 2012-13, are adult, responsible and free humans right from birth in many ways, whose sole purpose is to live out and to realize their individual Dharma. And their life mission/Dharma is simply to act out their spiritual truth in the physical life here on Earth and thereby integrate spiritually loaded physicality into society across the world.

Neither the Crystal Individuals nor the Crystal Humans that Crystal Individuals develop into later on, aim to save the Earth. Instead, they are here to increase the frequencies and the consciousness level to enable all people to help themselves. When you as a Crystal Individual and a Crystal Human have all the answers within yourself regarding your own life and your own Dharma, why would you seek external help to do things that you have the potential to do yourself?

The idea is for all Crystal Individuals to build up networks for their family, friends, hobbies and profession, i.e. social networks of various kinds, so that they can crystallize in their external relations in the very same way they are crystallized in their body and aura. Thereby, they will develop gradually into becoming more whole as Crystal Humans and have an opportunity to gather all the professional and human expertise through their Crystal network as well as any energy support they may need in order to follow their very own Crystal path in life.

In reality, there are not many things to be said about living a physical Crystal life, as both the urge of Crystal Individuals as well as Crystal Humans to follow and live out their own truth in life is all- consuming in their respective everyday lives. So, depending on what the Crystal Individual's and the Crystal Human's individual truth aims at, this truth determines how they live their lives, in which good timing is equally important.

In addition to the need for living out your inner truth at 'the right time', all Crystal Individuals' and Crystal Humans' lives are loaded with exactly those qualities that the New Time Karma consists of, i.e. respect, balance, justice, boundary setting, consequence, gathering and disseminating information as well as social and personal responsibility. This is why New Time Karma is an active element in each Crystal Individual's and Crystal Human's Dharma. And it is the very presence of these qualities that will help create committed, visionary humans on this Earth in the future. Humans who are not here to learn, but each in their own way contribute to enhancing the human standard regarding consciousness.

Such a life may seem extremely boring to people, who are not yet crystallized, as it sounds very structured and like a lot of hard work with no room for pleasure - but do not be fooled. In addition to having something meaningful and/or intelligent to devote themselves to, Crystal Humans really appreciate entertainment and experiences that broaden their horizons or touch their hearts.

Adult and young 'Crystals' prefer entertainment where the director was able to create an extremely vivid and/or grand atmosphere in his or her movie or theatre production. They also love stand-up comedy, in which the artist must possess a certain degree of intelligence to be able to identify the many things and circumstances that are being made fun of for the entertainment of the audience.

In addition, experiences in nature have a great place in Crystal Humans' hearts – and mean a lot to the entire consciousness system in their body and aura for that matter, as they recharge even better by spending time in nature. So, in many ways the life of Crystal Humans is not much different from that of others, as the life ingredients are largely the same. The only difference is that Crystal Humans are more conscious about why they do the things they do, and what their general objective is in a given situation. They consequently have the general outline of their life under control and are good at transferring this knowledge to the things they do in their everyday lives. So, everything in their lives fits together from an energy perspective and follows their general truth in life. In addition, they are good at setting big partial goals in life, even if their overall life mission feels a bit overwhelming at times.

Regarding Crystal Individuals' and Crystal Humans' life mission/Dharma, not all people have one single big life task deposited in their body cell structure. There may easily be several small missions on top of each other, or in continuation of each other that must be lived out and realized when the timing is right.

In comparison, the life missions that people at Indigo and Soul level have vary from the life missions and Dharma at Crystal level, and which are generally of a more personally committed character, where those involved each have something they

are dedicated to and are expected to contribute to the world.

Naturally, this happens at Indigo and Soul level as well - just not for everybody. At Soul level there is a learning aspect involved in most life missions that are connected to people's karma, e.g. they may each have something to learn in this life. The life missions at Indigo level by contrast often have a more rebellious character in order to shake up society and the immediate environment.

The topics that were included in Crystal Humans' karma and life mission while they were at Soul level might be transformed to their individual Dharma at Crystal level, i.e. Spiritual level. Therefore it seems as if those individuals are not yet rid of their karma, although they are. On the other hand, the personal lesson they learned at Soul level forms part of their Dharma at Crystal level where their mission is to teach the acquired knowledge to others. So the topic may be the same, but the approach to the life mission is not, as there is a big difference between being a student and a teacher in any situation.

In the everyday lives of Crystal Individuals and Crystal Humans, it is a high priority to be in balance at all levels as well as in relation to those people that are important to them. You do not spend time thinking about people who do not mean very much to you and who do not show any interest in you as a person. Crystal Humans spend their time cultivating those interests that support their current dispositions in life as well as support their further journey in life. This is not to say that they are only friends with whoever can help them on their onward journey, as they are just as likely to be friends with those they like to spend time with and where there is some sort of a human or consciousness match. Of course, the greater the match, the greater the urge to be in touch with each other where communication might as well happen via the Internet at a physical distance of 7,000 kilometres, but with full consciousness present, as it might happen over a cup of coffee at a café in the big city.

All Crystal Humans are very focused on being able to act as independent individuals who, deep down, are independent of others, but who at the same time respond well in the company of others. Their focus on the wholeness is just as big as it is on the individual, and not only on themselves as individuals. They also focus on each individual in any group context that they are part of, so in a way you could say that their attention is aimed in all directions at the same time.

At Crystal level it is extremely important for parents to know that their children can get by on their own here in life – naturally with great support from home – which is why early on in life, they teach their children about the value of focusing equally on themselves as individuals while also focusing on the wholeness around them, with the advantages of mastering both scenarios in life.

Children and adolescents must learn to both thrive and function in their own company, as well as that of others, regardless of the number of people who are present. Similarly, it is of great importance to Crystal parents that their children understand life and its mechanisms and they therefore spend a lot of time discussing various topics and life circumstances, until the parents feel confident that the children and adolescents have understood the things they have discussed. These parents therefore make an extra effort to ensure that their children and teenagers can get by in the prevailing society in a balanced way and that they practice a certain insight into social factors that are of relevance to the young people in particular. In addition, a balanced behaviour for children and adults is highly prioritized in Crystal families, at home as well as outside the home.

Crystal Humans are 100% focused when they work and are preoccupied with something of interest to them. In addition they help and support 100% those people who are close and dear to them when needed. At the same time, they are good at being in several places in their thoughts at the same time, although it may not always appear that way. You see, their minds are constantly working to find solutions as to how to improve conditions for themselves and others – often in reverse order – where they think of others first.

Their mental consciousness is consciously activated and switched to 'on' if they decide to work on finding a given solution for a particular situation. On the other hand, they are also very good at completely unwinding and turning their consciousness to 'off' if they need to relax and recharge. They then almost disappear from the Earth's physical surface without the environment noticing, because Crystal Humans can consciously activate as well as deactivate their physical visibility, without turning off the entire system.

In the New Time, money is a means of balancing to settle the sale of goods and services between people, especially between people with no prior knowledge of each other, which is a principle that Crystal Humans agree with. A moneyless society is therefore not at the top of the wish list in the Crystal Period, but rather belongs at a later consciousness level.

However, if it is a matter of compensating for human, physical and/or consciousness services between people who know each other, and that can be settled differently than through money, this way is preferred as has always been the case here on Earth when it comes to helping people close to you.

Crystal Humans are sensitive to various kinds of electro-magnetic frequencies (EMFs) from PCs, mobile phones, etc., but at the same time most have the ability to turn off the radiation impulses if for some reason they must be in places with plenty of radiation for an extended period of time. Crystal Humans are also good at subsequently balancing any imbalances and at removing any overload from their system, if they have not already protected themselves against the imbalance/overload ahead of time by surrounding themselves with physical devices that are capable of eliminating the damaging radiation.

Crystal Individuals and Crystal Humans are very conscious about their liquid and solid diets, which naturally allow room to party and enjoy various culinary delicacies. Generally, they eat a light diet that incorporates plenty of salads, vegetables and fruits of various sorts and little or no meat, and they drink very little or no alcohol, and the alcohol will mainly have a cleansing or relaxing function in their bodies.

In addition, many Crystal Humans focus on supplementing their daily diet with various strengthening, balancing and vitalizing health products, such as oils, nectar, essential salts and sugars, vitamins, minerals, trace elements and especially herbs, which the majority of Crystal Humans love. You see herbs have a strengthening and nutritious effect right down to cell level in the Crystal body and vitalize the Crystal body more than most other nutritional sources. Perhaps because herbs grow at earth level and have an earthly spiritual-physical coding that corresponds to the coding of a balanced Crystal body.

For thousands of years, herbs have been known for their nutritional, culinary and medicinal attributes, which is why their story speaks for itself, and the Crystal body really likes herbs as a dietary supplement and as part of their daily cooking. However, although Crystal Humans are extremely truth seeking and health oriented by nature, they are not fanatic about their diet or their lifestyle at all. Instead, they follow their body barometer when deciding what type of food to eat at a given time.

All Crystal Humans are naturally focused on having a balance in all aspects of life, but fortunately, that is not the only thing they are passionate about. As mentioned earlier, they are very preoccupied with their inner truth and therefore focus on ethics in their daily lives. In addition, they are also preoccupied with integrating qualities, such as love, aesthetics and beauty into all aspects of life and pay a lot of attention to their personal hygiene, their children's and that of their everyday environment. In fact, they rarely take the time to think about their partner in this respect, as one must assume that he or she has the exact same attitude towards hygiene.

Aesthetics and beauty are particularly easy to spot in Crystal Humans' interests in clothing, personal care and interior decorating, etc., as they always like to surround themselves with beautiful things of aesthetic beauty and a sense of purity. These qualities, however, are also very easy to see in their relationship with their partner where love, balance, aesthetics and beauty in the relationship are valued higher than anything else. In their relationship, sex takes a mixed first and second place, as sex is perceived as a natural continuation of the couple's love for each other. Read more about this in the chapter 'Relationships of the New Time' immediately after the case.

Case

Aura Mediator™ Louise Holmstrøm, a 34-year-old woman from Denmark, talks about her 'reverse' Crystallization Process:

My story is very simple and easy to understand, but also very complex because of the endless choices, possibilities and challenges I have been faced with and still am facing in my daily life.

For me, everything has happened so quickly, which is probably why I am different from so many others. I often meet people who have been searching spiritually for years, and who choose an AuraTransformation™ as sort of a last resort. It was my first choice and over a period of only five months, I was aura transformed as well as trained as an Aura Mediator™.

My Aura Mediator™ warned me that I might experience physical discomforts during my Crystallization Process, and I actually started to doubt whether she had performed the transformation properly, as I felt absolutely nothing! The only thing I noticed were the small glints of light in my aura, as if a sparkler were constantly lit.

Anni (Sennov), however, assured me that the work had indeed been done according to the book – I was merely 'in reverse'. As I used to be a competitive athlete, my body was better geared towards the Crystallization Process, so it was my aura that was 'staggering'.

Towards the end of the Crystallization Process I have experienced that my diet has had a great influence on my well-being. I have always had a sweet tooth, but my body now reacts severely to sugar. I cannot consume very much before getting a bad stomach ache. My body acts like during pregnancy – at times I crave certain foods, always from the produce department. I have pulled vegetables from the shelves at the supermarket that were foreign to me and, once I got home, I had no idea how to prepare them, which has prompted many unique and unusual dishes. I rarely feel like eating meat, which used to be a permanent ingredient in my dinner.

Psychologically, so much has happened. My intuition has increased tremendously, but I have been met with scepticism in relation to my 'gut feeling' and for a while, I doubted if it was right of me to follow my own intuition. I felt that it was extremely difficult to feel something so strongly inside of me while living in a world, my world, where I had to defend and explain my strong conviction all the time. Throughout the entire process, my husband has been a very good listener, to the best of his ability I might add, and has been supportive of my decisions. However, it is no secret that he has found it difficult to understand me, as his perception of the world is much more black and white.

Over time, my husband has opened his eyes to the effect of the New Time Energy. He has been an observer with a front row seat and seen the fantastic bond between my children and myself, which is now even stronger. However, we have also experienced that the gap between us as husband and wife – and as parents – has grown bigger and bigger. At times, it seemed as if our values were suddenly headed in opposite directions. My patience has been tested many times and I have been close to going crazy from his old, slow energy and we have both doubted whether we were even suited for each other.

In times of adversity, the children reacted by only coming to me and my 'luxury energy' – they couldn't use their father at all, and it has been extremely difficult to be holding the fort on my own and frustrating for their father to be of no use as he really wanted to help.

Halfway through my third pregnancy I had a strong feeling that this wonderful child I was carrying, should be born by Caesarean section (in Scandinavia, Caesarean sections are the exception, rather than the rule), and I really met resistance. The system, doctors, midwives and my own husband persistently tried to convince me that it wouldn't be good for any of us, that it was surgery that involved risks, incl. re-surgery and the paediatric ward. I fought for my belief and argued to the best of my ability and finally, I was able to break through a doctor's energy field and persuaded her to approve a Caesarean "on request of the mother".

My husband accepted it. However, up until the day when our little 'Crystal' was going to see the light of the day, I feared that he wouldn't forgive me if something were to happen to the child. Once again I doubted, as I wasn't even able to explain to myself why it was so important to have a Caesarean. When the day arrived, everything was perfect – except for the waiting time – which was quite long when you're waiting to meet another one of your beautiful creations. In the operating room, the anaesthesia worked right away and, before we had a chance to ask how long it would take, our little wonder screamed at the top of his lungs. He was simply perfect and definitely didn't need to spend any time in the paediatric ward, which I had feared up until then. I have never been happier.

As it turns out, the Caesarean wasn't just good for our little new boy, the entire family benefited from it. My husband developed stronger bonds with the two older brothers and, rather than being the spare tyre of the family, he suddenly became the one keeping the whole family together. As you can imagine, I was somewhat handicapped after the surgery and indeed I did need re-surgery, but it was worth it all.

Then one day my husband decided to become aura transformed as well. He wasn't completely convinced of the effect, but he wanted to – if not for his own, then for the kids' sake.

I had high expectations of the time following my husband's AuraTransformation™, which, for both of us, was an eye-opener that held a lot of exciting potential. However, I was deeply disappointed. I had expected him to now have the same view of life as I, but had to realize that he had to go his own way. And I had thought that all our obstacles and blockages would disappear immediately, but it was more like the bridge over our gap had been blown up.

My oldest son of four, who up to then had been an almost pure Indigo Child, reacted strongly. Previously, he had been able to take example from his father, but now it seemed as if he felt betrayed, almost abandoned, as if he could trust no one within miles. For about three weeks I was a witness to and part of a chaos, which I found it difficult to comprehend and handle. But then slowly things started to improve. My son's Crystallization Process suddenly took off and he found calm and new energies.

My husband underwent a Balancing session and spent a couple of months finding his standpoint in the New Time Energy and the bridge over our gap was repaired and then became redundant – because – in some strange way, we reconnected because of what this is all about, namely our love for each other, our family and life.

We are still very different and do things in our own way, but with the same values and objectives in mind. Our respect and love for each other has grown to unimagined heights, and our children have really benefited from having two parents who are on the same wavelength.

We have noticed that our social circle has changed. Friendships that were mostly based on need, started to fizzle out without a sense of deprivation, and new relationships and friendships packed with positive energy have popped up 'out of the blue'.

When I think back and turn it all upside down, the Crystallization Process has been an outstanding experience and an eye-opener to a different world. I have been part of such chaos while possessing an inner calm and belief that there is a meaning to it all. I have felt in my own body how adversity helped me to develop, so that my ability to listen to and feel my body is now top notch. During the process I have been confused and lost faith in my own abilities, but have ended up believing in myself and acknowledging that each of us is special and is able to do something special – we just need to remember to take responsibility for our own lives.

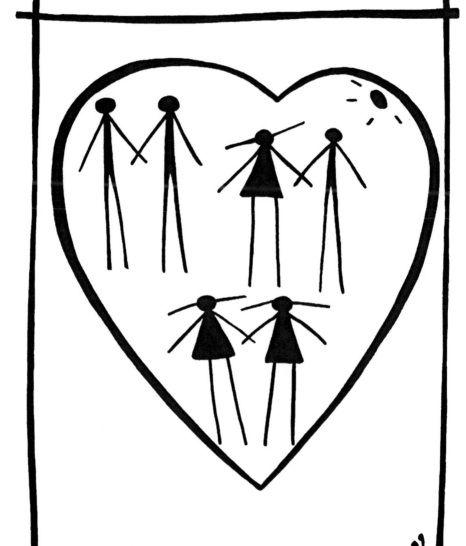

"ALL KINDS OF LOVE ARE LOVE"

Relationships of the New Time

Within the Crystal Energy, love and balance together is the number one priority in a relationship. In addition, sex has a natural place in the relationship, which is actually not talked about that much. You see, in the Crystal Energy it is perceived as extremely uninteresting for most people to be following each other's sex lives, unless the parties have the same special sexual preferences.

Crystal Humans are simply not interested in, whether their environment is heterosexual, homosexual, bisexual, transvestites, androgynous or whether they have undergone sex change surgery or belong to yet another group of people.
Nothing interests Crystal Humans less than hearing about how others have sex. They would rather enjoy the experience themselves with their partner, without involving anyone else, in order to focus their energy and the experience around the couple in unison. For Crystal Humans, sex acts as a pure elixir of life for both the body and the mind.

As long as adults do not have sex with children or animals or cause any harm to their sexual partner without his or her consent, they are free to do anything they want sexually in the future. In the Crystal Energy, however, we will be seeing a strong tendency towards Spirit mates, with similar consciousness foundations in spirit, being brought together at the physical level.

> Spirit mates, not to confuse with Soul mates, have identical consciousness structures because of their common source in the spirit, where they originate from the same cosmic cell division. On their way from the fogs of the Universe towards this solar system and on towards the Earth, cells always divide into two cells at a time that, together, represent spiritual dualism. It thus becomes possible to create a physical attraction between two similar individuals - here on Earth and elsewhere in our solar system.

The more the spiritual dualism gains ground on Earth, the more we will see earthly relationships fall apart, if these are not based on respect, openness, honesty and safety above all. In the Crystal Energy, real words are put on the table, so if one party gets turned on by unfamiliar partners out on the town, and the other party gets turned on by the money and prestige the couple enjoys together, then this is how it is, and neither of the parties will doubt for a minute. There is therefore no foundation for prostitution in the relationship and pretending to be ignorant about a partner's out-of-town affairs because of fear of losing the joint home through a possible divorce.

Therefore, a bad conscience - where one party puts financial pressure on the other or pushes the other party beyond their personal limits, because he or she has a skeleton in the closet or wants to do anything to save the relationship - can no longer be used as physical commodities. Similarly, it will not be possible for one of the parties, who may feel that he or she is 'loved too much' by their partner, to use their partner's love to manipulate them to their own advantage. Such condescending behaviour is simply not part of the New Time relationship structure, as they are not part of a Crystal Human's energy structure.

> Spirit mates have a lot to learn from each other, as they often have completely different earthly life experiences, and if there

are problems in the relationship, these are always caused by circumstances in the couple's exterior environment, such as children, extended family, work relations, etc.

If the relationship is perceived as complicated, the parties are definitely not each other's Spirit mate and, for your information, it is possible as an individual to fully crystallize in your aura and your body before meeting your Spirit mate.

If there is too much light and therefore Spiritual Energy in a relationship, it will harm the physical attraction between the parties. In any earthly relationship, whether it involves Spirit mates or Soul mates, it is therefore important for the relationship to constantly focus on balancing energy, rather than on pure light energy. You see, pure light tends to blind its environment, so that the parties do not see each other as physical beings, but rather as allied spiritual beings that do not always need to practice physical interaction with each other.

Throughout the years I have encountered several spiritual couples that were unable to sleep near each other. They might be able to sleep apart with their own (spiritual) light fully activated in the system, but if their partner had his or her spiritual light activated as well, the room would simply be too bright for any of them to fall asleep in each other's company. In such instances, the brain is unable to find rest and both the brain and the person feel tortured by the joint light – and in reality mostly by their partner's light – which seems like an external, distracting element that completely destroys the person's inner balance, which leads to a lack of sleep.

The same thing applies if one party has a large amount of spiritual light and the other party does not. In that case, the most physical of the parties will have their sleep interrupted, unless he or she completely closes their personal blinds to their partner's spiritual light.
If the physical party does not close their personal blinds and keep a focus

only on their own energy, he or she will get burned from an energy perspective by their partner's strong spiritual light instead, which may lead to an increased thirst in the most physical party. However, water is not always the drink that is consumed to compensate for the high temperatures in the spiritual partner's energy. Earthly-oriented people often choose to consume large amounts of alcohol instead in order to counteract the partner's strong Spiritual Fire.

The above-mentioned process indicates, in every way, how important it is for the two parties in a relationship to have a pure energy balance in relation to each other. Their time together will then be a giving experience for both parties and at all levels, rather than one party constantly trying to deliver a certain kind of energy to the other, which he or she cannot consume, and vice versa.

When aura-transformed people enter into a relationship with non-transformed people, it often entails a noticeable, physical imbalance in the relationship for the transformed party.

The aura-transformed party may not necessarily pose a potential fire danger for his or her non-transformed partner, i.e. a risk of the non-aura-transformed party's Soul aura being consumed by fire. On the other hand, the transformed party often has to push his or her partner to think and act faster to match the energy of the transformed party. The lack of energy match is mostly felt and experienced by the transformed party when the parties have had sex together, as he or she then feels totally drained of energy, while the other party feels completely re-energized.

Relationships between Soul mates are often based on a mutual balance between the parties, where they take turns helping each other get more energy by giving some of their own energy. This helps maintain a mutual balance in the relationship, which rarely strengthens both parties at the same time.

In a relationship between two Spirit mates, the parties also help each other increase their energy, if need be, but this happens by each of them copying energy from each other, as it is done by Crystal Individuals and Crystal Humans, which you can read about in my book 'Crystal Children, Indigo Children & Adults of the Future'. This enables both parties to be strong at the same time, as neither will drain their personal energy pools when helping their partner increase his or her energy. This is because each party's respective energy pools remain in their own camp, and they feel strong and collected in their respective, personal energies, which is of great advantage when the copying function is initiated.

During the copying, both parties copy each other right down to cell level, so that all energy and new registrations, which each party may have made during that day or since last time they were together, are transferred internally between the couple. This is a process that often happens automatically, especially at night when the couple sleeps next to each other, when they walk hand in hand or when they make love.

So although an AuraTransformation™ helps the individual balance him or herself and subsequently body crystallize, it is deeply rooted in human nature, and therefore also in the body consciousness that the two parties in a relationship are expected to help each other in any situation by exchanging energy with each other. This exact equalization act, which at Crystal level is a copying act, makes many people feel physically and energetically attracted to each other. When at some point they feel satiated by the partner's energy, many often seek a different appetizing energy, until some day when there are no outstanding energies left for them to integrate at a personal level.

If an aura-transformed person who has reached full balance in his or her life is physically intimate with a non-transformed person, it is natural for the transformed party to take over some of the counterpart's imbalances to work on these in their own balanced system. Correspondingly, it feels completely natural for a non-transformed party to take on half of their partner's balanced energy in their system as if it were their own – and who benefits the most personally from such an arrangement in this situation?

Naturally, the non-transformed person does, and the aura-transformed person then has to spend time getting rid of the counterpart's imbalances in his or her system, which is not fair for either party. Unfortunately, the fact that the aura-transformed person accepts to take on his or her partner's personal imbalances in their system does not always help the non-transformed party gain permanent balance in their life because often these imbalances recur with a vengeance shortly afterwards, as the person has not learned to process his or her imbalances.

Fortunately, most aura-transformed people instinctively know that sex with a non-transformed person automatically involves a reduction of their physical energy. This is why many aura-transformed people make the 'difficult' decision to not have sex with anyone at all, until the right partner shows up. So, the fact that many aura-transformed single people choose to lead a celibate life, rather than having sex with the first one they meet whose energy matches their own to a small degree, is really a consciousness 'survival mechanism' that helps them maintain a consistent high frequency in their body and consciousness.

For a while, my Danish Facebook group 'Krystal-netværket' (The Crystal Network) had a discussion titled 'New Time Love' where I made the following statement about sexuality in New Time relationships. It should be noted that I am not making a statement based on pure imagination, as I live in a relationship with my Spirit mate, in which the following is an established part of our physical intimacy:

"To me, the advantage of being body crystallized and spiritually enlightened right down to cell level in your body, is the very fact that the Spirit is always an active part of the sexual act as well as of all other aspects of your life. This is why performance and potentially lower impulses are never allowed to control the process that naturally involves the physical body, which benefits from an orgasm at various levels.

From personal experience it is just as natural in a New Time relationship to have sex as it is to have lunch together, etc. and often the parties have sex in order to balance themselves in relation to their partner, e.g. if they have been apart for a few days or if they are in two different physical spheres during the day. It is sort of a physical-spiritual fusion in the relationship that, in a very simple way, ensures that both parties read each other's energy and balance each other's energy without too much explanation.

My experience has taught me that there is no need for Tantra in the same way in New Time relationships as previously, as the parties do not need to hold on to their own, respective energy. Instead, it is about equal exchange of energy and no suppressed release to the benefit of your own body and mind. Everything is divided equally between the couple."

Case

"Life can be like a concentration camp or an amusement park. The deciding factor is your consciousness level."

By 49-year-old, Norwegian Isilia Holmøy, who is an Aura Mediator Instructor™ in Sweden:

I compare auras with cars, and I really feel like I have advanced from an old, used Lada (the old aura), through a mid-size BMW (the Indigo aura) to a brand new Porsche (the Crystal aura)!

When I underwent my AuraTransformation™ in 2004, I didn't know anything about it. A lot of things happened in the time after, which didn't feel particularly good to be me. I didn't realize the connection until a couple of years later when I read the book *'Crystal Children, Indigo Children & Adults of the Future'*.
At the end of 2007 I became a certified Aura Mediator™ and even ended up with an improved balance myself.

Previously I had meditated and worked a lot with light; I had completed the Oneness University program in India and learned to give Deeksha/Oneness blessings. After a while, I had an increasing sense of discomfort in my body. The symptoms involved an intense burning sensation in my spine, brain and heart, a feeling of having a sunburn inside that made me crave a lot of water and frequent baths and showers, tightness in my chest, 'snow blindness' in the mornings (it felt like sand in my eyes), unusual fatigue that made me want to sleep all the time, and migraine-like headaches where no painkillers would help. I saw my doctor and a neurologist and was told that there was nothing wrong with me.

But I felt mentally empty and it was difficult to think clearly, my memory got so bad that I started to worry, it became very challenging for me to stay grounded and I experienced a violent restlessness/vibration/irritation inside my body, as if the frequency of the molecules in my body had been dramatically increased. This made it impossible to relax and I started having cramps, especially in my legs, so I couldn't sleep. My partner felt the disturbing vibrations and moved to a different bedroom. In the end, it felt like my entire body was infected like rheumatism, with stiffness and aches in my muscles, tendons and joints. I discovered that it helped to stretch carefully, but when things were at their worst, I had to stretch for about an hour, just to be able to get out of bed in the morning, and often I needed a warm bath, before feeling fairly well. I also had hot flashes and had to put on and take off my clothes throughout the day and I started having night sweats. I often cried of exhaustion.

It all made it challenging for me to live and it took away much of my joy. However, the worst thing was that my clients started to display the same symptoms and that was the last straw for me. On the advice of Anni (Sennov), I closed out the light energy/(and) the Deeksha energy and focused on the balancing energy. It felt like a drastic step and I had to think it over for a couple of weeks, but I haven't regretted it. Almost immediately after, I was overcome by a wonderful cooling and soothing sensation inside of me. It became nice to be in my body and I was able to relax again. I immediately felt grounded and balanced. It was a huge contrast to the light energy. My body temperature is steadier now, my feet are no longer as cold and many little disorders have disappeared.

One morning I had a clear intuition that I had too much acid in my body. I changed my diet, so that the following week, I only ate basic foods and I started to feel an improvement after a couple of days. After one week my pain and stiffness was almost gone. I have now discovered a base-forming powder that is quite effective. At the same time I started taking supplements of fatty acids as a vegetable oil mix and it felt like my body was thrilled.

Food: I now recognize what my body wants and *doesn't* want, which has lead to quite a few changes. I crave more fresh fruits and vegetables, eat less meat and ready-made food. If I have too many dairy products, I can develop resentment towards these.

I don't really like alcohol and can't drink very much, either. I sometimes still long for coffee and chocolate. The coffee shops are so nice and inviting and the shelves with candy in the stores with their poisonous cocktail of sugar and chemicals have grabbing arms. This urge, however, is mental – my body doesn't need it at all.

Other than that, I feel like exercising more and am much better at taking time out to rest. My body also really appreciates the extra oxygen it gets through some easy breathing exercises and I enjoy being in nature more now than I used to.

I'm more relaxed regarding financial matters now. It is no longer difficult for me to charge people for my work and I can afford more. It seems that the subconscious programming I used to have, which claimed that it is not spiritual to earn a lot of money, has been erased in me. I call this collective program 'The Camel Virus' according to the quote from the Bible, "It is easier for a camel to pass through the eye of a needle, than for a rich man to enter into the Kingdom of Heaven." Back in time many things were loaded with a certain amount of guilt, insecurity and bad conscience, but now things are neutral. In fact, it feels as if the entire world is neutral, including myself, which makes it easier to live, as there are no inner conflicts.

I discovered that I had an energy/consciousness that didn't belong in my energy system - an energy **parasite**. It felt like a claw in my back between the shoulder blades, it weighed heavily on me and my back lost all its energy. It stole all my energy. I carried it around for a long time before learning how to clean my human energy system of something like that.

When I close my eyes now, my body feels like pure flowing energy. Often, happiness bubbles through my body and calm gratitude flows. I feel grounded and present and clearer in my mind than I have been for a long time. It simply feels good to be in my body now.

I have been given *healing power* and now work with this full-time and I have also discovered other capabilities that I didn't have before my AuraTransformation™. I can look straight through people's masks and understand why they are the way they are and why they do as they do, I see subconscious programs and mental prisons that people have, concepts of thought/systems of faith that make people feel captured, and their strategies of energy manipulation. I recognize the blockages or the constrictions of the energy flow in people's bodies with sometimes-unpleasant accuracy.

The intuition from the Spirit comes to me as 'multi-dimensional information packages' that sort of arise from the bubbles from deep inside of me and, once they reach the surface, they crack and provide me with spiritual knowledge. The information is comprehensive and the understanding is deep, like wisdom.
If out of old habit I run myself over by following the will of others, my body clearly puts its foot down - it is as if it yells "NO!!!!". If there is something I really feel like doing, my whole body sings and I get lots of energy.

Once in a while I get a strong intuition and I sense a tremendous force flowing through my body and I then feel that there is nothing I can't do. It's a strange feeling to feel the intuition from your body, rather than from your mind.

I no longer let anyone manipulate me, as I see energy games and hidden agendas so clearly. I dare to say what I mean and have acquired the ability to say it in a way that creates the least objection and doesn't hurt. I used to have great difficulty saying no in an honest way. It is now easy – there is no bad conscience.

I now have great *self-confidence* and perhaps that is what I'm most happy about as it enables me to relax and be myself without any worries. I feel free. The only times I feel a little insecure is when I meet people with very poor self-confidence, as I can relate to their feelings. I can relate to what others feel and think and whatever suppressed emotions they might have, but this is not a problem for me anymore.

It now feels as if my *heart* is in my entire body, not just in the chest like before, and I feel larger than before, as if I am reaching beyond the boundaries of the physical body.

My *sex life* has totally changed. I am so much freer than before, so that everything is more relaxed, full of enjoyment and, sometimes, laughter. I have experienced feelings and conditions that I had no idea existed and I feel everything within and outside my body (not just my lower body). I feel that it is appropriate to introduce a new concept: *The New Time Orgasm*.

Although I believe that 'we are all one' at one level, I have grown very conscious about my personal energy, which I have at my disposal on this physical planet. This enables me to consciously distinguish mankind's personal or collective energy (misery) from my own energy/condition, and I sense if anyone tries to invade me, control me or take away energy from me, either through personal contact or from a distance. This makes it easier for me to stay mentally and emotionally, even physically, balanced.

Manifestation: It is now much easier to attract things that I want. I am experiencing many incidents of miracle-like 'coincidences', which have given me a feeling of 'gliding through life on a banana peel'. When life somehow goes against you, I don't see it as a 'problem', but rather as a 'challenge'.

The AuraTransformation™ and the Crystallization have made me thrive here on Earth. I am enjoying more and look forward to the future.

Use your Crystal Energy constructively

Since the relationship between Crystal Humans' thoughts and spiritual consciousness and their physical reality is completely matched, what goes on in their minds and their physical lives is naturally synchronized. This is a fact that is not yet clearly visible within society in the years up until 2012, as there are not yet many fully crystallized Crystal Individuals and Crystal Humans. However, the closer we get to 2012, the more evident this correlation will be around Crystal Humans.

Crystal Humans take great interest in society and environmental issues, as well as other people and human development in general. It is therefore difficult for them to stay calm if there is a need for assistance, development and improvement in their immediate environment.

In reality, Crystal Humans have a high-frequency and eternally moving Spiritual Energy that lies dormant inside of them. This energy causes them to take action almost every time they register a thought impulse, or if they are told that there is a need somewhere for spiritual progression comprising mental and/or physical improvement and development.

To ensure that all the world's Crystal Individuals do not have to fight their own little personal fight in life more or less in solitude, things are set up so well that the next step in the great Crystal plan is for each Crystal Individual to create a Crystal network in society. By socializing with equals in a variety of ways, they can then be upgraded to Crystal Humans who are not only crystallized in their aura and body, but also in their environment.

It is therefore important for all Crystal Individuals to establish social relationships and to join various networks, such as interest and study groups, sports teams and social networks and naturally, personal networks related to friends and family, etc. Whether these networks involve aura-transformed people or not is not really of great importance. What matters is the objective of each network.

Facebook, for example, has become a great hit in many countries where people meet through the Internet to exchange knowledge and experiences with each other and to be able to follow, although somewhat at a distance, the lives and interests of their Facebook friends, whether these be friends, relatives, current or old school mates, colleagues, neighbours, friends of your children, various business contacts, etc.

When each Crystal Individual has instigated various initiatives to create their own social, private and/or professional Crystal network, it is important to also focus on helping your close relationships to become upgraded with respect to their energy as well. This is because, what good is it, if your partner, your children, your immediate family and friends are all at a different consciousness level than you and do not balance well in their respective lives? In that case, Mr. and Mrs. Crystal will gladly jump in to help their environment obtain a better balance in their lives. You see, this is a prerequisite for them to be able to crystallize in their own consciousness, unless they have decided that it is impossible for them to help one or more people close to them obtain individual balance at Crystal level.

In the Crystallization Phase as well, once you are fully crystallized, it is important to be conscious about the energy you surround yourself with, both professionally and personally. It is thus important to return all energy to people you have spent time with in different contexts during the day, as well as pulling back all your own energy to yourself. This is because Crystal Individuals tend to commit themselves 100% to people and causes they are dedicated to, which is absolutely fine. However, it is important to only be dedicated to the cause when you are 'on' – not necessarily when you are somewhere else far away from pertinent people and need to re-charge.

I recommend doing the exercises in the book *'Den Bevidste Leder' (The Conscious Leader)*, written by my husband Carsten Sennov, to help you manage your own energy on a day-to-day basis if you feel that your life is not quite under control. The book contains the entire daily energy repertoire that people who are crystallizing need to use during their Crystallization Phase as well as once they are fully crystallized.

Although I helped write some of the chapters of the book that deal with the four element profile™, which is a personality type indicator based on the four elements of Fire, Water, Earth and Air, I wish I had written the whole book myself. It is so specific that anyone can understand it, regardless of his or her consciousness background.

To avoid summing up the entire content of a book that has already been published, and a book that contains everything about managing your personal energy, professionally and personally, I have selected two exercises from the book that are about pulling back your own rightful energy to yourself as well as returning the energy of others:

Exercise – Pull back Your Personal Energy

It is recommended that you do this exercise in a quiet place at first and make sure that you have at least 15 minutes, free from interruption at your disposal.

You need to decide, whether you wish to:

1. *Pull back all your energy in general, or*
2. *Pull back all your energy from a specific situation, person or place*

If you wish to pull back your energy from a specific situation, person or place, you will benefit the most by selecting the situation, person or place that has been most draining for you, as this is undoubtedly where most of your energy is tied up and can be pulled back home.

Once you have made your choice, you can begin the exercise.

Make sure that you are sitting in a relaxed position.

Close your eyes, take some deep breaths and let your breathing calm down while you focus on your task.

Then mobilize all your will and power without tensing up your body. Only use your mental power while doing the exercise.

Now imagine that you enter a fight in which you pull back all your energy to yourself from a person, situation or place.

It is important that you imagine pulling back the energy through a cleansing filter, before it comes back to you, so that you ensure that you receive only your Personal Energy.

Continue this until you are either tired or sense that it is time to stop.

Stay seated and relax completely. Let the calm spread throughout your system again.

Once you master this exercise, which you should be able to relatively quickly, you can do it anywhere and at any time. A couple of minutes are often enough, but naturally this depends on the amount of energy that needs to be pulled back from the particular situation, person or place at the given place or time.

The exercise can also be done on behalf of others, but only if:

1. *You are responsible for those people, and if*
2. *They are incapable of doing the exercise themselves, e.g. young children*

Exercise – Return the Energy of Others

As in the previous exercise, it is recommended that you do this exercise somewhere quiet to begin with, and that you have at least 15 minutes at your disposal.

Decide whether you wish to return the energy of others in general, or whether you wish to return only the energy of a specific person, situation or place.

Once you have made your choice, you can begin the exercise.

Make sure that you are relaxed. Close your eyes, take some deep breaths and let your breathing calm down.

Now mobilize all your will and power without tensing up your body. Only use your mental power while doing the exercise.

Now imagine searching through your own inner system and your consciousness for the energy of others, other situations or places that should not be there. You may have taken the energy consciously or subconsciously, willingly or unwillingly.

Now imagine that you find something that you wish to get rid of. By the force of your mind, you return this to its original owner, situation or place. You then continue the search within your system.

Before returning the energy, you have to cleanse all the energy to ensure that everything sent off has been cleansed of your Personal Energy.

Continue to do so until you are either tired or sense that it is time to stop.

Stay seated and relax completely. Let the calm spread throughout your system again.

Once you master this exercise, which you will relatively quickly, you can do it anywhere any time. A couple of minutes are often enough, but naturally this depends on the amount of energy that needs to be returned to the particular situation, person or place at the given time.

You will most often do this exercise in continuation of or in connection with the exercise 'Pull back Your Personal Energy', which it is logically connected to.

The exercise can also be carried out on behalf of others under the same conditions as described in the exercise about pulling back energy.

This exercise may be done when needed, particularly when you have been close to people or been in situations or places where you know that negativity is directed towards you. This exercise can also be beneficial if you feel uncomfortable or if you feel a negative energy in or around you and/or your environment.

It is also recommended that you do the energy exercise if you suddenly notice that you are reacting or thinking differently than usual, as this might be because you have taken on the energy of others in your personal sphere.

If you wish to learn more about similar and related exercises, I recommend reading the entire book *'Den Bevidste Leder'* (*'The Conscious Leader'* – currently available in Danish only), which you can read more about at **www.good-adventures.com**. The book is directed at everyone, whether they are at Soul, Indigo or Crystal level.

Case

42-year-old Aura Mediator™, Trine Zoe Eriksen, from Denmark, describes her personal Crystallization Process as follows:

I was aura transformed over Easter in 2007. After my transformation, the biggest cleansing happened in my love life, which went from one extreme to another several times over the following six months with the father of my children, who became transformed two weeks after me.

In October 2007 I decided that it was finally over between us. At the end of December 2007, however, I decided to go back to him, as I realized that he is the only man who makes me feel at home and that, in spite of our problems, nobody at all compares to him. We haven't been apart since, although it has been turbulent and I have felt like leaving several times.

In March 2008 I became a certified Aura Mediator™.

In the summer of 2008 - for the sake of the family - I decided to focus on my family, particularly our children, who had suffered during our arguments and I asked the Universe for help.

In September and October 2008 I was completely useless each day when I came home from work. I had absolutely no energy – only enough to get by. My children's father and I were both very dizzy during this time and I was very thirsty. During a conversation with the Aura Mediator Instructor™, Sofia Liv Ebling at the beginning of November 2008, I learned that energy-wise, I had spent the last two months pulling up my children's father to approximately my level and that this was why I had been so drained and we both reacted by feeling dizzy and thirsty. Since then, the family has been able to relax more as a whole.

During the process, my two daughters have been balanced a couple of times and they have leaned on me almost the entire time. They have felt more or less in symbiosis with me. My son, on the other hand, has mostly leaned on his dad, which has really surprised me, as my son is of very high frequency and therefore was "supposed" to lean more on me. This has happened more over the last few months, though, since I have settled more into the Crystal Energy; he wants me much more now and leans more on me.

Physically, so much has happened. I was never a big drinker. I completely stopped drinking alcohol two months after my AuraTransformation™. Much has changed in my diet as well. I stopped eating mammals in January 2008. In July 2008 I stopped eating poultry. I actually don't have a problem with eating animals, as it has always been a natural part of the food chain. But my body just doesn't want mammals and poultry anymore. I now sense much more clearly what my body needs than I used to. Sugar doesn't agree so well with me anymore. I get a rash around my mouth and on my chin when I eat sugar and am starting to refrain from eating that as well, although I find it hard. I am getting help from a hypnotherapist to fight off my sugar cravings.

Since my transformation, I have had Vega tests done to see what my body needs and have cleansed my body with various products. Through a Vega test I discovered that I am very sensitive to electro-magnetic frequencies (EMFs), particularly flat screens, laptops and mobile phones. I now carry a Mini Rayonex with me wherever I go and sleep with it under my pillow at night. It eliminates the harmful rays and its effects. I have also tried various diets to cleanse my body.

I have taken and still am taking vitamins and minerals every day to keep my body as healthy as possible. I have found out how my body works best. This happens when I do the Five Tibetans 6-7 days a week, drink plenty of water, eat lots of fruits and vegetables, get plenty of protein and healthy fatty acids, sleep 6-8 hours a night and otherwise live a relatively healthy life. Due to my work I bike 100-150 kilometres a week, which my body enjoys. I also try to swim at least one kilometre a week. Water is a wonderful, freeing element for me.

I have never doubted my mission in this life. I have always wanted to help others on their way. I am in my 25th year of working within the health industry. I have always carried out my Care and Nursing assignments with a view to helping others to the best of my ability and in a way that I would want to receive help if I were in their situation.

I was always interested in the alternative world. In 1995 I became a reflexologist, in 2000 I became a Reiki healer and in 2005 I became a Craniosacral therapist. From 2006 I worked as an alternative therapist at a clinic a couple of days a week, which I really enjoyed. After my AuraTransformation™, I was suddenly left with no energy to treat others, which is why I stopped giving treatments at the clinic. This lasted for about a year. I spent most of my time sorting out my own energy and everything that that entailed. When I started giving treatments again, people came to my house and my treatments improved. It was as if I were on a roll without having to think too much about what to use in my treatments and which techniques to apply. Today, I feel that everything has fallen into place.

During my regeneration phase I still needed something to live on, and for a number of years I have been registered with a temp agency, which was ideal for me. Thankfully, since I had been in the business for so many years, I didn't have to worry too much about my work, as I knew everything by heart.

Today, things are flowing more smoothly and are falling into place. However, I sense that my 'helping gene' is running thin, as I have been very focused on taking responsibility. One thing you are sure to encounter within the health industry is elderly and sick people who often find it difficult to take responsibility for their own lives and the consequence of their lifestyle. They often say that society or people around them are the reason for their unfortunate situation. I now prefer to tell people the truth – in a way that they can understand - rather than paying lip service. In my opinion, they are better served this way. I sense that I give rise to many thoughts with my colleagues when I tell them about some of the people I help to look after.

One of the big topics within my psychological and social life has been manipulation. I have had a couple of great 'teachers' while growing up and also in my adult life. Since my transformation I have worked intensively to address those manipulation issues and am now so sensitive to it that I watch my prey like a hawk whenever I encounter manipulation in my everyday life.

Throughout my life people have made use of my energy. I have also often taken responsibility for other people's lives and squandered my energy. In addition, I have been carrying my family's energy around subconsciously for several years. Of course this has really drained me and at times I slept a lot. Since my AuraTransformation™ I have been very aware of pulling back my own energies and returning the energies of others. I have worked a lot with this process and actively used the book *'Den Bevidste Leder'* (*'The Conscious Leader'* – currently available in Danish only). Since November 2008 it has not been necessary for me to pull back my own energies and return the energies of others. Slowly but surely the need stopped by itself over of a couple of months.

As for relationships in my life, I was never one to have lots of friends. Throughout my childhood and my adult life, I have had a few, close friends with whom I could have deep conversations. Concurrently with schooling, education, interests and moves, some friends have been replaced. Over the last couple of years, some of the friendships have ended and new ones have arrived, all of which has happened as a natural process in my life. I have, however, been puzzled by many people close to me as well as distant relationships over the past few years. At times, I have been very frustrated by some people and have had to withdraw from them.

In those instances it was about taking responsibility as well. They either expressed that others were to blame for their present situation – or they had difficulty taking responsibility for the consequence of their own actions. Therefore, I couldn't respect them and had to withdraw from them, as I felt that my energy level decreased whenever we were together. Today, I have peace, regardless if people take responsibility for their lives or not.

I know for certain that we are all exactly where we are supposed to be and we learn from life as we can, at the right time and place. I now know who I am and what I'm supposed to do with my life. I don't need to get confirmation from anyone and I am comfortable with myself.

The consciousness dimensions and the four elements

The 1st, 2nd and 3rd dimensions belong to the Soul Energy and correspond to the development process that has existed for people on this Earth for the past millennia.

The 4th dimension represents the transition, also called the Indigo Bridge, between the Soul Energy of the 1st–3rd dimension and the pure Spiritual Energy at Crystal level in the 5th dimension. It is in the 4th dimension at Indigo level that AuraTransformation™ originates, where it is possible for people, through an AuraTransformation™, to erase their karma and the consciousness baggage in their aura that has its origins in their past and any previous lives at Soul level.

The 5th dimension represents the Spiritual Crystal Fire Energy.

The Crystal Fire causes people to genuinely burn within their heart, and this in turn compels them to follow their inner truth in life and to do what feels right for them, at any cost - human, social or financial.

The 5th dimension is the first phase on the way towards becoming a spiritually and physically balanced Crystal Individual of the 9th dimension – and in the 5th dimension it is possible for Spirit mates to begin the fusion of their respective Spiritual Energies.

During the transition from the 4th-5th dimension, the three Chakras – the Hara Chakra, the Heart Chakra and the Forehead Chakra are combined into one big Heart Chakra that belongs around Thymus, and the Indigo aura's frequency is increased and thereby automatically transformed into a more Spiritual Crystal aura.

In the 5th dimension it is Fire - the will and commitment to a purpose, as well as learning the truth in each context - that is the leading element of life. It is therefore also important to integrate the following dimensions: the 6th dimension's Water element, the 7th dimension's Earth element and the 8th dimension's Air element, so that the Crystal Energy can take on a more tangible, visible and measurable form in the aura and the body.

In the long run, it is not a very satisfactory situation for the majority of spiritual people to be involved with many things and at the same time be fighting to integrate Spiritual Energy on Earth – simply because they are in the 5th dimension's Spiritual Fire element, which is equivalent to the first phase of the Crystallization Process. The Individual should also preferably be taking joy in doing the things they do, as well as having an individual objective or purpose in life that stimulates them, which is achieved by also integrating the 6th, 7th and 8th dimensional energies into their consciousness. In this manner consciousness automatically continues to flow into the 9th dimension's Crystal Individual Energy that brings with it the feeling of being an independent individual capable of cutting off and separating yourself from other people's thoughts, emotions, energies, etc. This is where you are able to act as a freethinking and free-acting spiritual individual experiencing wholeness on the earth plane for the first time.

The 6th, 7th and 8th dimensional energies make it possible for the Spirit to really be integrated into the aura and the body in crystallized form, thus avoiding the risk of burning up in the 5th dimension's pure Spiritual Fire Energy. The Crystallization of the 6th-8th dimensions' Water, Earth and Air Energies, however, is a very slow process that can take many months, even years, for the body to complete.

The 6th, 7th and 8th dimensions deal with our personal skills and abilities and living out our personal life mission, and these dimensions help open up the body consciousness, so that our Crystal life mission in the 9th dimension can be exposed as a coherent and clearly-defined mission that we can relate to with our full consciousness.

The 1st-5th dimensions are described in detail in my book 'Crystal Children, Indigo Children & Adults of the Future' of 2004, which is why I am choosing only to describe the 5th dimension's energy here. The 5th dimension represents the first phase of the Crystallization Phase on the way towards becoming a Crystal Individual of the 9th dimension and later on a Crystal Human of the 13th dimension. In addition, I am going to briefly discuss the elements of the 4th dimension to offer an insight into the transition from the 4th-5th dimension.

To clarify, I have made the following illustration that shows the 1st-9th dimensions and the elements associated with each dimension. When you read on after this chapter, I recommend that you revisit this perspective from time to time, in order to better see the energy context between the dimensions, in this case seen from an earthy perspective.

Please note that you may come across comments on energy dimensions that are described in a completely different way than the one mentioned here, which means that the dimensions that someone is referring to are not earth related.

Dimensions and Elements

9th DIMENSION = CRYSTAL INDIVIDUAL ⇒ FIRE

Phase 1: to establish a Crystal network in which the Crystal Individual, in addition to FIRE of the 9th dimension, must integrate WATER of the 10th dimension, EARTH of the 11th dimension and AIR of the 12th dimension – in order to be able to move on to the 13th dimension and become a full Crystal Human.

6th dim	7th dim	8th dim
WATER	EARTH	AIR

5th DIMENSION = CRYSTAL BEING ⇒ FIRE

Must be integrated into the aura and the body
= Phase 1 to become a Crystal Individual

4th DIMENSION = THE INDIGO BRIDGE

FIRE = 5th dim
WATER = 3rd dim
AIR = 2nd dim

WATER = 3rd dim
AIR = 2nd dim
EARTH = 1st dim

SOUL ENERGY:

3rd dimension: WATER

2nd dimension: AIR

1st dimension: EARTH

In the 4th dimension, the *1st dimension's grounding* = Earth, the *2nd dimension's balancing energy* = Air and the *3rddimension's love energy* = Water, are all transformed into a joint unit of energy consisting of *air-based balancing energy* (originally based in the 2nd dimension), *water-based love energy* (originally based in the 3rd dimension) and *fire-based Spiritual Energy* (based in the future 5th dimension).

People's original grounding, balance and love energy are therefore upgraded to a higher-frequency energy consisting of balance and love at Spiritual level, rather than balance and love being considered from a purely earthy perspective.

Energy-wise, the 4th dimension's Indigo Energy is a mix of energies from the Old Time and New Time Energies, respectively, which is why it is appropriate to describe the energy as the Indigo Bridge that separates and/or connects the old and the new world.

Once you have moved across the Indigo Bridge into the New Time's pure Spiritual Energy of the 5th dimension, the final consciousness choice has been made and there is no way back to Soul Land.

The 5th dimension is controlled by the Fire element, which is the primary and fundamental energy at Spiritual level. Consciousness wise, the 5th dimension's Fire element makes us truly burn in our hearts, while the strong Fire Energy in our bodies, which primarily burns in the legs and the lower part of the abdomen, provides good grounding and personal drive in life.

The 6th dimension's Water element, the 7th dimension's Earth element and the 8th dimension's Air element act as independent consciousness dimensions in continuation of the 5th dimension's Fire element.

These three elements are each as important as the Fire element and can be developed and integrated separately.

The order of Fire, Water, Earth and Air represents the optimal order for each individual's development and integration of the four elements because the order makes us act out our Dharma and Crystal life missions within the 9th dimension's Crystal Individual Energy in the right way. In this context, it is very important to truly burn in the heart as well as constantly following your inner truth. Unfortunately it is possible to burn in the wrong way, which is why the truth aspect has been given the ultimate first place in the dimension order together with your personal drive. Both abilities originate in the 5th dimension's Fire Energy.

In addition to the Fire Energy, it is important to have the 6th dimension's Water and the New Time's flow within yourself, to douse and curb the all-encompassing Crystal Fire from time to time. The Water element enables you to follow your inner flow and intuition and stay calm and keep your energy to yourself if you sense that your way forward is not clear.

For crystallizing humans, things should flow preferably in a positive way and have good timing, which is the Water element's great force. They are therefore able to maintain detachment from unbalanced situations, to identify themselves with other people and situations and create a furore if it feels right to react intensely in a given situation.

Like animals of the sea, they use their inner sonar system to orientate themselves in relation to the surrounding world. They are extremely good at orientating themselves in respect to the proximity of 'danger' and/ or the unknown, and will usually refrain from acting on the perceived threat until they are fully informed about the scope of the danger and/ or the unknown energy. They therefore never judge from a distance, but always open up to creating flow and balanced collaboration with others.

When the future Crystal Individual is capable of burning properly in his or her heart and follows their inner flow, it is time to put things into physical shape using the 7th dimension's Earth Energy. This energy thus represents the forming force that enables future Crystal Individuals to realize their inner truth in a balanced way in the outer physical world.

Last but not least, it is important for future Crystal Individuals to gain insight, an understanding and to establish a perspective of their life situation and their future tasks. It is for this reason that the Air element is not developed and integrated until the 8th dimension, as the last element before the transition to the 9th dimension's Crystal Individual Energy.

Although we as humans have to move into the 9th dimension to have our Crystal life mission exposed, many of us can have several life missions within one or more dimensions, all the way back to the 1st dimension. And only once our life mission has been revealed to ourselves do we feel inspired to move back to the exact dimension where our very own life mission belongs, which we are then expected to act out and follow through.

If the Dharma and life mission of Crystal Individuals and Humans belongs to the 1st dimension, they are meant to help people survive or move away from the survival stage.

In the 2nd dimension Crystal Individuals and Humans work in the bank, insurance and medical industries as well as with balancing body treatments, etc. Here, Crystal Humans help others maintain or regain their physical balance in life regarding their finances, their home situation as well as their physical body, etc.

In the 3rd dimension Crystal Individuals and Humans are therapists and caregivers – either independent or within the health sector, personal wellness and in daycare facilities where they are responsible for daily care and help to build up the psyche of people.

In the 4th dimension you will find Crystal Individuals and Humans whose mission it is to turn the structure of a company or an institution upside down. They possess destructive as well as constructive abilities while having the courage to go against the collective consciousness, even though both their feet are solidly planted in the collective consciousness in their everyday lives.

In the 5th dimension Crystal Individuals and Humans are leaders and entrepreneurs, etc. who thrive when following their inner goals and leading others. These people possess an active driving force, which they constantly access in order to reach new goals either by themselves or together with others, e.g. their colleagues. They consistently burn through old paradigms with the power of their convictions.

In the 6th dimension Crystal Individuals and Humans consciously choose to help others, similar to those people of the 3rd dimension. In this case, however, it is an attempt to follow their individual goals and callings in life, without asking too many deep questions about the situation. People with a life mission in the 6th dimension are very dedicated to their calling and thrive on the things they do in life.

In the 7th dimension Crystal Individuals and Humans have settled as artists and have managed to show their inner truth in a visible form. In addition, this category includes sales people and messengers of all kinds, who have consciously dedicated their life to communicating information about a certain topic, a certain lifestyle or religion, etc.

If people of the 7th dimension can vouch for a product or a message, they truly know how to 'sell sand in Sahara'. It is therefore important for them to have the 5th dimension's Fire Energy and the 6th dimension's Water (intuitive flow) in place within their consciousness before they begin to act out their life mission in the 7th dimension. In the Crystal Energy, it is very important to have ethics in place so that sales people and messengers ensure that the product and the message match the needs of the relevant recipient at all times.

In the 8th dimension Crystal Individuals and Humans act as trendsetters, creative visionary think tanks and promoters of new initiatives, such as advertising, marketing, projects, inventions, research, activities and trends – even new lifestyles.

In the future, the 9th dimension will experience many Crystal Individuals and Humans who, in their daily activities use all four elements of the 5th-8th dimensions. However, their main focus will be on the Fire element and the urge to make their ideas burn through in society. They may be all-round mentors and advisors for others and initiators of personal development forums, centres and meeting places for others looking after all aspects of physical and spiritual, personal development at the same time.

The 9th dimensional life missions are not yet particularly widespread within society, but clearly we will see much more of these in the years to come.

Since there are still too many unresolved issues regarding the life missions of people here on Earth in the 10th-13th dimensions, I am not going to touch on that here. However, there is no doubt that the life missions will concern relationships that reach beyond the individual and certainly involve cooperation, development and holistic thinking at relationship, family, company and society level, respectively.

As mentioned several times earlier, the Crystallization Process in the aura and the body leads people through the four elements of Fire, Water, Earth and Air, which all belong in the 5th-8th dimensions.

Once an individual is fully crystallized in the 5th-8th dimensions, he or she becomes a Crystal Individual of the 9th dimension, able to begin realizing their life mission, which is exposed at Crystal cell level within the body in the 9th dimension.

Later on, the individual continues to crystallize in their social network and becomes increasingly holistic, through which he or she develops into a Crystal Human of the 13th dimension.

A Crystal Human is a person of the 13th dimension who completely focuses on the individual and the wholeness at the same time and who has both aspects under control in his or her life. This means that this particular individual has an inner balance, is centred within their own body, and also has an outer balance that is expressed through the aura. In addition, the individual has a positive social network in a variety of contexts, both personal and professional alike.

A Crystal Individual is a person of the 9th dimension who, so far, 'only' has the individual energy under control and who is fully balanced within themselves and aware of their individual goals. Many children of this type are being born from 2009 and onwards.

Children of the 13th dimension, on the other hand, will not be born until around 2012-13. In relation to adult Crystal Individuals and Humans, there is therefore a big difference in how far each person has come in their individual Crystallization Process and in their journey towards becoming a fully balanced Crystal Human of the 13th dimension, which naturally affects the way in which they live their lives.

For example Crystal Individuals who are in the 9th dimension may get bored in the company of others if those people are not at the same consciousness level as they are themselves. These people will not have that experience, once fully crystallized in their 9th-12th dimension network energies. Once they are realized as Crystal Humans of the 13th dimension, they will then be much more conscious about what they face in any given situation and adjust their consciousness to the appropriate level in advance. Therefore they do not risk having a lot of high-frequency energy armed, locked on and ready to be fired off just below the surface of their energy system towards people that they will never be using their ammunition on anyway. It is much better to leave the energy weapons at home, so that they are ready for use at some other time when it makes more sense. Crystal Humans of the 13th dimension know how to choose their battles.

Crystal Humans are much better prepared to meet their environment at a consciousness level than Crystal Individuals. Fully crystallized Crystal Humans are much more accepting of others - regardless of their consciousness standpoint in life – than Crystal Individuals, who have only just sorted out their individual Crystal Energy and therefore want to meet the world on their own consciousness terms.

It is possible for everyone to develop the energies of the 5th-9th dimensions in their consciousness, regardless of whether they have undergone an AuraTransformation™ or not. However, it is not possible to make your Crystal life mission visible in the 9th dimension unless the energies have been developed in the right order, i.e. Fire, Water, Earth and Air and this is where the big consciousness development dilemma arises. Once you have let go of your Soul aura and have unintentionally moved into the 5th dimension's Fire with your aura and your body, it is incredibly difficult to control the flames to such an extent that you are also able to develop and integrate the Water element to balance the Fire. This, however, is much easier in the body than in the aura as the body consists of approximately 70% water.

Unfortunately, I have encountered several clients who were very hard hit by cancer and who did not make it through the 5th dimension's raging

Spiritual Fire. These individuals were not sufficiently protected and balanced in their aura to be able to resist the full presence of the pure Spirit in their aura and their body. Unfortunately, at the time that I met them it was far too late to change their consciousness situation.

You see, pure Spirit ranks alongside death in the earthly universe. It definitely also does for the physical body if the pure Spiritual Fire Energy is allowed to take over, without balance and in relation to the physically dense body energy. This is why it is so incredibly important during the Body Crystallization Phase to constantly maintain focus on a balance between the Spiritual and the Body Energies because, no matter what, it is an extremely difficult time to have to experience the physical symptoms of illness as a result. In reality, you are in the 5th dimension and feel physically much more dead than alive, while the Spirit is very much alive. It is therefore good to have some 6th-dimension Water Energy, 7th-dimension Earth Energy and 8th-dimension Air Energy to fall back on and to balance out the Fire Energy, if you were lucky enough to develop those qualities back in the 1st-3rd dimensions at Soul level. Therefore, everything is good for something here in life, as everything is connected and has a greater meaning!

In the 1st-3rd dimensions, all adult Soul Humans have had their first chance to develop a more physical variation of the Earth, Air and Water elements, respectively, and in the 6th-8th dimensions they get a second chance to develop these same elements and qualities at a Spiritual level. In other words, you could call it energy recycling, in which case the energies are constantly moving upwards and outwards in an ever-growing spiral, away from the dense, earthy physicality towards a more spiritual goal.

Case

Aura Mediator™ Anneli Heintz, 52-year-old woman from Denmark, talks about her Crystallization Process:

I was aura transformed in May 2007 and already four months later I was connected to the Crystal Energy (author's comment: *this happened as part of the Aura Mediator™ training*). I am still in the process of crystallizing. The first phase was about disassociating myself from old systems. I quit my job within the public sector shortly after being transformed and stopped working just before getting connected to the Crystal Energy. I had a very strong feeling that I wouldn't be able to deal with the hierarchy and the heavy energy. I also ended up having a huge argument with my, otherwise, good colleagues.

I am now able to work there as a substitute once in a while, but when I do, I am not subjected to the system in the same way. My relationship with others has changed as well. Some of those I knew before my transformation now keep a certain distance between us (although they don't know that I have been transformed), but I get along great with people that I have met over the past six months, although they are not transformed.

I have no problem being with friends and family - however, not for too long at a time - and I have also become good at choosing whom I 'feel like' talking to and I close down when the talk/topic is too much about old times.

I thrive when I'm with children and adolescents, and children who are completely unknown to me like my energy, e.g. at a party when kids seek me out. It also happens at the supermarket or at the mall where children reach out for me or make eye contact – they totally light up.

My relationship with my son, who was born in 1998, is out of this world. He has a lot of Crystal Energy. The day after my transformation, he really started to read and once I had been connected to the Crystal Energy, his math work improved tremendously - he now starts to do his homework as soon as it has been assigned. He sometimes starts to feel ill if he doesn't start his homework right away. I feel that we have a great mutual understanding, so the conflicts between children and adults that I hear are going on in other homes are unknown to us. It sounds rosy – and it is.

My daughter, who was born in 1984, has a lot of Indigo Energy, so she actually shouldn't have been born until 1991. Up until just a few years ago, however, I knew nothing about these things, but I always felt that the energy she had was the 'right' one. When I was transformed she was in New Zealand, but she called in the middle of the night to tell me that she had met a girl whom she had fallen in love with, but that there were some problems as well. So, all the way on the other side of the Earth, she felt that I had received her energy and that she could now involve me in her personal life – it was fantastic! Since then, my daughter has been aura adjusted and has settled in New Zealand and since we are connected through the same energy, we understand each other very well despite the long distance.

Physically, I crave to become as clean as possible e.g. I have had all my amalgam fillings removed, which left me with a sense of relief, physically and psychologically.

I have also changed my diet. I have reduced my consumption of meat considerably – I now only eat meat once a week, such as chicken and a little beef. I eat a lot of fish. At the moment, I eat porridge in the morning to achieve as much balance as possible. I drink coffee, as I like the taste, but no more than 2-3 cups a day, after which my body automatically says stop. I drink plenty of water, which I always have, as well as green/white and red teas. I still enjoy a glass of good red wine.

I take large doses of vitamin C and Omnimin and, at times, Royal Jelly. I drink Aloe Vera every morning and use Aloe Vera products for my skin and body. I sell the products myself.

I particularly crystallize behind my ears and inside my ears and for the last six months I have had pain in my right shoulder and right side of my neck. The pain is caused by the activation of my DNA and some feelings that I am slowly feeling ready to deal with and act out.

I really try to stay physically balanced by mountain biking in the forest and doing yoga. I have felt very tired at times and have also had periods of feeling down and on the verge of tears.

My relationship with my husband has changed as well, which is difficult. He has always been very understanding of my alternative views of various things, but the higher and stronger my consciousness gets, the harder it gets for us to reach each other, which makes me feel lonely at times.

Over the last month I have had a strong feeling/knowledge that I need to have a numeroscope done in order to have the energies adjusted in relation to myself and right now, it should have been yesterday (author's comment: *In January 2009, Anneli changed her name from Anne*).

Another physical disadvantage is that during my Crystallization Process I have hit menopause, when body and mind change as well. When I act completely according to whom I am, I only have mild symptoms of menopause. So, being the way I am and liking it when things are under control, there is a lot of work to be done. I know that my development happens really quickly energy-wise, but yet I am often frustrated that the development in those whom I associate/speak with is so slow and that they are having a hard time moving forward.

Whenever I am really in 'the New Time Energy' I have an incredible sense of calm in my entire body that fills me completely. The calm is throughout me - a calm that others can see as well. Once I have this calm integrated permanently at some point, I believe that my Crystallization is over. 2008 has been a year of much learning/understanding for me, as it was a year influenced by the Air element. In the 2nd quarter, I had to be close to water, which is why we bought kayaks. In the 3rd quarter I spent a lot of time in nature and slept in a tent to stay grounded, and in the 4th quarter I spent a lot of time 'lying fallow' in order to integrate the knowledge I had gained throughout the year.

2009 has started out with much energy and optimism – and I know that this is the right path for me.

(Author's comment: *2008 was the year in which the 8th dimension's energy really reached Earth. In the 1st quarter, the focus was on the integration of the Fire element, in the 2nd quarter on the integration of the Water element, in the 3rd quarter of the Earth element and in the 4th quarter the focus was on integrating the Air element).*

Expression of the elements in the New Time

At Soul level, Fire Humans, who are 5th-dimension spiritual beings deep down and not yet capable of expressing their rightful Spiritual Energy in a balanced way, primarily express themselves through passion, aggression, commitment and periodic outbursts of 'the moment of truth' when they lay out everything on the table.

At Spiritual level, 5th-dimension Fire Humans use their Fire instead to burn all inconvenient relations and conditions out of their lives that no longer feel right – often without analyzing the situation first.

They simply base all their decisions on their gut feeling about how things should be in order to feel right for them.

At Soul level, Water Humans of the 3rd dimension have difficulty separating their own energy from that of others, which is why they too often become overly emotionally involved in their fellow humans and let themselves get carried away by general reactions in the joint consciousness. Therefore, it feels perfectly natural to them to, e.g. cry at the death of a public figure, even though they did not know that person personally.

At Spiritual level, Water Humans of the 6th dimension, on the other hand, are observant and intuitively perceptive, which is why they are good at sensing danger as well as relating to other people's lives and situations without flowing along in their own energies. New Time Water Humans have their very own balanced energy stream that flows just as well on its own as it does in unison with those of other people.

At Soul level, Earth Humans of the 1st dimension have practical minds, are stable, have stamina, but are not particularly versatile as individuals. At Spiritual level, Earth Humans of the 7th dimension always rate their environment, situations and projects from a holistic, physical point of view and they primarily evaluate their fellow humans by listening to their opinions and observing their behaviour.

At Soul level, Air Humans of the 2nd dimension often subconsciously try to impress each other with their respective knowledge which may stem from a variety of sources, such as magazines, newspapers and books as well as the Internet, lectures, gossip, etc. Conversations, humour and knowledge sharing are highly prioritized but they do not always view the world at Earth level, rather from a bird's eye perspective.

On the other hand, at Spiritual level, Air Humans of the 8th dimension perceive others as a whole and observe their energy field without being aware of this themselves. They do not need to have their observations confirmed as they, like Sherlock Holmes, have all details under control while keeping a good perspective.

New Time Water Humans like to be seen, enjoyed and generally be able to affect their environment through their mere presence, whereas New Time Air Humans like to be seen and appreciated for their intelligence and great knowledge. New Time Air Humans often have many thoughts at play in their minds, without others noticing this, and they are always either one or ten steps ahead of everybody else regarding preparation and planning.

New Time Earth Humans really want to be appreciated for what they have produced and like artisans and artists, they take great pleasure in showing their physically visible and/or audible creations to others. New Time Fire Humans just want to reach their goals, which may sound a little narrow-minded, but nonetheless is a huge accomplishment in itself, as they often set high goals in life.

If the need to follow and act out your inner truth were not the 'leading star' in the New Time Energy, we would run the risk of many Water Humans mistakenly mixing their pure Water with Earth Energy, in the hopes of creating a physical flow – often resulting in mud. The idea is for both Fire and Water to move into Earth in order to create a spiritual flow physically, but not until the Fire burns properly in the stove and the energy stream flows in a truthful way. In this context, it might be worth considering whether we wish to create flow exclusively to make money and keep society going – or do we need to create flow to help others become gradually more conscious?

In the New Time Energy it is okay to earn money through physical flow, as long as the intention of the flow is good and meets the criteria of the New Time Karma. The fact that Air is the last element is merely that all knowledge, wisdom, insight and debate of various kinds, which belong in Air Land, is only relevant if it carries a spiritual impulse that can be converted to physical form. Words and research for the sake of words and research alone mean absolutely nothing in the New Time Energy.

If people's Water element is stronger than their Fire element, they often find it difficult to understand why they cannot simply go with their inner flow. Often there is a small fight going on inside them between those two elements because the Water must acknowledge that it is the truth of the Fire that runs the show and that the Water cannot just flow as much as it would like to. The idea is for New Time Humans to first and foremost live and act according to the highest impulse, naturally taking into consideration their personal wishes.
Water Humans, who have yet to integrate the Fire element into their consciousness system, often prefer to float around in their very own vibrations and energy, without any specific purpose.

People with too much Earth are rarely good at recognizing their own psychological needs and those of others. However, they recognize when their physical needs awaken and this type of person often experiences very tangible confirmation that the Spirit has occupied their person and their life. This often happens as actual miracles, which are really spiritual eye openers. Alternatively, they do not understand clearly enough that the physical world is not the only world there is.

In the old days, the Earth element of the 1st dimension was the deciding element in humans. It used to be, and still is in some primitive societies around the world even today, that people let themselves be guided by their body's needs and are under the direct influence of the physical Mother Earth. Unfortunately, the Air element of the 2nd dimension was not as developed back then, which is why Earth Humans of the 1st dimension did not feel particularly inspired to actively change their physical conditions. This does not mean that they were unintelligent. They merely possessed an earthy intelligence controlled by nature that enabled them, like animals, to join the life cycle of Earth, and accept the physical conditions.

New Time Crystal Humans, on the other hand, are capable of controlling their own bodies and actions themselves through the four elements, which is why it is so important for them to have balance in all their elements.

The Fire and Spiritual Energies of the 5th dimension are far less structured and more drastic than the Water, Earth and Air Energies of the 6th-8th dimensions. Therefore, it can be both extremely positive and extremely dangerous for the community since it cannot be controlled in the same way as the Soul Energy. The expression therefore depends on each individual's degree of consciousness and of the individual's compassion, intuition, personal flow and ability to balance in his or her own energy within the Water element of the 6th dimension. It also depends on the individual's visibility, creative ability, formulating ability and manifestation power in the Earth element of the 7th dimension and, last but not least, of the individual's physical as well as spiritual knowledge level in the Air element of the 8th dimension.

Not until all four elements are developed and integrated into each other does the Spiritual Energy take on a much more balanced form in the 9th dimension than it did in the 5th dimension.

As a very important element in the individual's consciousness in relation to others, a final balance between light and darkness is created in the 8th dimension, i.e. between the Spirit and the matter, when the light takes the lead and ensures that the darkness can keep up. The spiritual teacher begins to take care of their earthy physically oriented student, who thinks that he or she can do most of it by themselves.

The gender problem is really balanced out in the 8th dimension, which I will try to explain in the following, and which can be related to homosexual relationships as well. The explanation, however, can just as well be applied to all men and women's unconscious behaviour in relation to other men and women from back in history and up until now.

The woman of the dark, who is very physical, resents the man, and the woman of the light, who is very spiritual, seeks him out. The man of the light resents the woman, and the man of the dark seeks her out, as she represents the other side of him.

The woman of the dark represents the masculine energy without knowing it and thus seeks out female company, as the man of the dark would have done. The man of the light seeks out men, as the woman of the light would have done.

When saying that one part is light in their energy and the other dark, it is really about opposite polarities consisting of Spirit and matter, respectively, which are drawn to each other in the earth's dimension. Only by identifying the fundamental core of consciousness in each human, which for women can easily be dark and light for men, through which they may be predisposed to enter into homosexual relationships – is it possible to activate the right polarity, so that Spirit mates can find each other, regardless of their gender.

The most interesting part of taking on the many dimensional shifts in connection with your Crystallization is that sometimes, it feels as if you live several lives in the same life. This can be felt all the way back to the Indigo Energy of the 4th dimension where, for the first time, it is possible to establish contact with consciousness on a daily basis, representing the term eternal life.

Each dimension represents a phase of life in itself, which can either be integrated in a few months or over several years, and during these respective phases, you may suddenly get close to some people whom you may never see again when you move onto the next dimension. It is also possible, however, to meet them again in a later consciousness dimension, when the parties have each integrated their energies, and are then again able to enrich each other in this later dimension.

If you would like to read more about the four elements I recommend reading my husband, Carsten Sennov's book, '*Den Bevidste Leder*' ('*The Conscious Leader*' - currently available in Danish only). You can also read about the elements at **www.fourelementprofile.eu** and **www.annisennov. eu** under 'Articles'.

Case

Aura Mediator™, Magne Botnedal, 55-year-old man from Norway, responded to his AuraTransformation™ and simultaneous Crystallization Process as follows:

I underwent my AuraTransformation™ in November 2006 and was most likely already in the process of crystallizing. To me, this was an almost euphoric experience, as it was truly a joy to connect with my own Spiritual Energy and to become more whole as a person.

At the time, I was already relatively focused on my diet and taking care of my body and mind, so it didn't lead to significant changes in that regard, but rather a confirmation that my lifestyle in this area was right for me. However, I now realize that it can be advantageous to take vitamin and mineral supplements and that this can help cleanse the body – so that is probably something I will do during the last phase of my Crystallization Process.

In general my life hasn't changed too much, although I'm probably more spontaneous now in many ways, I am clearer and choose more, according to what will bring me the most joy. It has also become much easier to say no to things that I actually don't feel like doing – in a balanced way, without hurting my environment. The biggest decisions during this period have probably been to live more, take more chances and to listen more to my heart than just 'common sense' – which has given me many exciting and wonderful experiences. In addition, I now find it easier to meet new people at heart level and to talk about what really matters, as I am much less inclined towards small talk.

It would be fair to say that life has become more precious to me during the process – I am more conscious about how I spend my time, with whom I associate and what I wish to learn from new experiences. Perhaps one of the best aspects is that I have met many new, interesting people during this time with whom I have had great conversations, experiences and challenges, all of which I cherish. In addition, it is now easier for me to accept when others have a different opinion from my own, choose differently than I do and pursue different experiences – without me feeling the need to have an opinion about it.

This again has led to me accepting that there are some things that I cannot change, but I am more active in situations when I can actually make a change for the better, both through work with energy, but also through many different kinds of intervention.

I must admit that I am a bit impatient by nature and have therefore made a conscious effort to crystallize as quickly as possible, although it has entailed many challenges. Of course, it is not always easy to know what causes what, as we are still influenced by planet energies and by our environment.

My experience seems to be that of feeling everything so much more intensely than I used to, especially when I have a close relationship with someone. Even the smallest thing becomes extremely intense and old patterns that have been repeated in my development process seem stronger than previously. So, a comment made about something, or a lack thereof, in certain contexts, are intensified, e.g. if I don't feel appreciated, affirmed or even loved – that is all very painful for me at the moment.

The pain doesn't necessarily last for very long and most often it is enough to do a small 'meditation' to cleanse my own energy and to give myself the love energy that I had expected from my environment. After that, I usually quickly regain my balance.

Another thing that I find challenging about this is that so many people around me have the Old Time focus, which I see reflected in them wanting to explain my processes with psychology, questioning techniques and anything to do with the mind. This is very frustrating, as I don't recognize myself in the picture they paint of me and I actually end up somewhat devastated and angry, as I am not viewed as a whole individual, but rather as a 'mind'. The farther I get into this process, the more I realize that only the language of the heart works for me. I cannot and will not be part of such mind games as they only create inner chaos. When this happens, I despair at first, but then always realize that this it the truth for others and by finding my way back to myself again, things fall back into place.

In addition to 'meditation', it helps me to go for walks in nature, particularly to one of my energy spots, which I have been working on to open up for the New Time Energy. When I go there and cleanse, work on letting the elements cleanse me, giving myself love and sending love to the current processes, I find that relatively quickly I become a newer and better person.

I probably thought that many of my imbalances would disappear during this period of time, but truth be told they are probably more visible and pop up in every situation with a lot of emotion and passion, especially in close relationships. However, I realize what it is all about much more quickly than I used to and it is thus easier to work it out, put it behind me and move on. Some of the processes look like repetitions anyway and keep coming back, especially during the times when the energies are increased here on Earth through strong planetary constellations and important dates related to energy, e.g. 08/08/08.

The advantage of these periods of increased Spiritual Energy, however, is that the Earth's energy points are easily accessible and it is then easier to work through more and deeper layers of old patterns and to come out on the other side more balanced than previously.

In addition, there is no doubt that the Crystallization is reflected physically as well, e.g. pain occurs in totally unexpected areas for no apparent reason; the pain usually lasts for just a little while, with only a few exceptions. In my case I have experienced persistent muscle pain, which can be a physical part of my repetitive processes that constantly remind me that yet more needs to be burned out. Since I have a strong Fire Energy I use this consciously to burn out anything old, sometimes with the help of the other elements as well.

One of the really good things for me about the Crystallization is that my Crystal aura has become much stronger, which has the effect that I take on other people's imbalances much less in a challenging environment, e.g. when people smoke or drink a lot. I have been more sensitive than most people I know in this area for a long time – something that is thankfully easier to live with now.

It has also been challenging to meet people with Old Time Energy, especially when they want to 'heal' me or treat me in a different way. If I don't manage to stop this in time, it usually leads to headaches or other pain and increased irritation. It is not always easy to explain to people who really just want to help you that this will indeed lead to the opposite of help. It works best for me to say that I have my own permanent therapists, whom I trust and use whenever I feel the need.

Meeting children, especially Crystal Children, has been the best proof of my actual change. I have a four-year-old grandchild who wants to spend more and more time with me and who really appreciates my energy and my presence – and needs it, as no other adults in her environment have undergone an AuraTransformation™. We have a great connection and understand each other even without words – and we really have a good time together. It's the same thing when I meet other children – they enjoy my company and it's extremely easy to connect with them, to the joy of them and me. I have always enjoyed spending time with children, but to be with a Crystal Child is a gift, as they are themselves 100% and show an honest, bubbling zest for life. I have noticed this with others who have undergone an AuraTransformation™ as well – the fact that children really want to connect with us.

Dimensions and spiritual dualism

When people let go of their consciousness baggage and karma at Soul level through an AuraTransformation™, they get closer to the essence of their inner consciousness.

The masculine and feminine energies are combined in their consciousness and they have now taken their first active step towards gradually approaching their Crystal life mission and their Dharma.

At the same time, they approach the energy and the person (with whom they originated in spirit) who is their Spirit mate; their other half and thus their opposite, but at the same time, their equal.

Love looks very different, in the Spirit mate relationship, from the one we know from 'ordinary' relationships. It may therefore be difficult to detect your Spirit mate at first, as the energies do not move about the way they usually do and we as humans therefore do not react in the usual way. The energy between Spirit mates works at a much finer, higher and at the same time deeper and broader level than in other inter-human and partnership relations. You cannot even have the same consciousness synchronization with your most beloved children, as they have their own Spirit mate somewhere out there with whom they fully match.

When people have moved through the 4th dimension's Indigo Energy via their AuraTransformation™ (if that is where they find their consciousness standpoint right after their AuraTransformation™), they continue their journey into the 5th dimension where it is possible to begin the fusion with their Spirit mate in earnest. Today, however, many people flow directly into the 5th dimension's Crystal Energy once they become aura transformed, as they do not need to stay on the Indigo Bridge of the 4th dimension as part of their consciousness development. They merely use the bridge as a consciousness passageway between the Soul and Crystal Energies and do not need to make a prolonged stop on the way.

The meeting and physical fusion between two Spirit mates usually does not take place in the outer world, until both parties have combined and balanced each of their inner masculine and feminine energies. A fusion that here on Earth belongs in the 4th dimension, but which can be integrated in Soul Humans at consciousness level right from birth.

It is therefore possible for a couple who have met already at Soul level to be Spirit mates as this experience will have given them an opportunity to help each other integrate the opposite polarity in the external world. Not many couples are granted this opportunity however. The couple cannot begin to activate their joint Crystal life mission, though, until they are both aura transformed. You see, it is not possible to ultimately determine, whether both parties are Spirit mates or not, unless they both undergo an AuraTransformation™, as this will make their respective consciousness potential and the cohesion with respect to their energies, visible.

The physical meeting between two Spirit mates opens up consciousness to the possibility of an energy androgynism and inter-sexuality appearing in both parties, as they will now be able to sort out their own masculine and feminine balance as well as those of their partner. This is an energy constellation that will, in the end, enable them to manifest their respective inner energies in the outer world, so that their joint Dharma can be transformed into a specific action. Once the couple's respective masculine and feminine energies have been equally integrated in both parties, they therefore no longer need to fuse with other people's energies to become even more whole than they are already. One could say that the parties exchange polarities, which then signals to the outside world that they are now fully occupied in a relationship.

When Spirit mates mix together their respective masculine and feminine energies, a new and even stronger consciousness structure occurs, which strengthens the two Spirit mates' personal power and charisma.

Before the Spirit mates meet on Earth, they pretty much develop together, so if something happens in the life and consciousness of one party, something similar will happen in the other party's life and consciousness.

One party, however, may be much farther along in their personal consciousness development than the other. This means that one party may not therefore be able to continue in his or her development until the other party has begun their personal development and does their consciousness work for the benefit of the Spirit mate relationship.

For example, there is a great difference in the parties' consciousness level if one party has been aura transformed and the other has not. However, the other party will move very quickly in his or her consciousness development and act relatively quicker than expected, as soon as he or she has been aura transformed. Through this process many imbalances between the parties are smoothed out relatively quickly.

If the Spirit mates are very far apart in consciousness when they meet, it can sometimes lead the parties to try to fuse with the 'wrong' partner because they meet a person who, from a consciousness perspective, is just as far as themselves. Unfortunately they do not belong to the same consciousness sphere and dimension, and this is called consciousness dualism.

The following briefly explains the three consciousness relationship constellations that we as humans know today:

Soul mates

`Soul mates` can be explained as an energy constellation between two fundamentally different spiritual beings who, for the sake of consciousness development on Earth, have agreed to follow each other as love partners throughout several incarnations on Earth. The Soul Energy, however, is abating, as all children born from 1995 and onwards are exclusively born with Spiritual Energy.

Consciousness mates

The resemblance in energy between Consciousness mates originates in connection with their personal development through life experiences here on Earth. This does not necessarily mean that they are identical in spirit. Any such relationship is different from the Spirit mate relationship as it is not always sexually and physically focused. You can easily meet several Consciousness mates on your personal development journey. These mates may be of either sex where the relationship appears to be either deep friendships or often brief and very intense love relationships that turn into nothing. The consciousness dualism solely represents a step in the journey towards spiritual dualism.

Spirit mates

An individual's Spirit mate corresponds to the other half of the Spiritual Energy with whom they originated at consciousness level long ago in connection with the great cosmic separation of cells. Each cell has always been divided into two, which together represent the spiritual dualism and this cell separation is being returned to its spiritual origin by bringing together the Spirit mates as love partners in their earthly lives. Spirit mates have the exact same consciousness structure and have a deep, sincere love for each other as well as an often-inexplicable sense of connectedness, which Soul mates and Consciousness mates do not experience.

The explanations mentioned here are taken from my husband's and my book 'Åndsdualitet – en bog om kærlighed' ('Spirit Mates – A Book About Love' – currently available in Danish only) of 2003..

Consciousness and Spirit mates can be difficult to distinguish, as they are far more synchronous with each other than Soul mates with respect to their energies. The quickest way to identify the relationship is therefore to observe how quickly imbalances occur in the relationship. You see, in the situation of Spirit dualism, it is extremely difficult to disagree about anything at all, whereas there are often small and big tiffs between Consciousness mates because of their different perception of things.

The Soul Energy and the consciousness dualism therefore only represents a small step in the earthly development journey, in the quest to become one with his or her total consciousness and pure Spiritual Energy and to finally be re-united with their ultimate Spirit mate in body and spirit.

When the time is right, the consciousness fusion between Spirit mates is simply unavoidable, which results in their consciousnesses flowing together into one spiritual mass, each maintaining their own body, so that after a short period of time, they end up appearing as two bodies and one spirit.

Two Spirit mates may very well have met and lived together already while they were both in the 1st-4th dimensions, but not until in the 5th dimension, do they have the opportunity to meld consciousness together in the physical dimension.

Depending on the Spirit mates' joint life mission, however, they may not meet each other at physical level until they have each integrated the Fire, Water, Earth and Air elements in the 5th, 6th, 7th and 8th dimensions, respectively.

For adult Crystal Individuals, meeting your Spirit mate is a very important part of building up your personal Crystal network. So, in addition to every Crystal Individual building up their own Crystal network in the 9th-12th dimensions, this is also where the Spirit mates have an opportunity to integrate their partner's Fire, Water, Earth and Air elements into their own aura and body.

If Spirit mates do not meet each other until in the 9th dimension, the consciousness fusion will not happen any earlier than this. The fusion will then happen much more easily than if the couple were connected in the previous dimensions, as they are now both fully crystallized individuals who have each defined themselves and their respective energies.

In the 10th dimension, the Spirit mates act as two bodies and one Spirit divided into two consciousness pools and auras.
Unlike before when the parties met at a physical level, they now each have a much greater consciousness experience pool to draw upon, as they will each have received a copy of their partner's consciousness experience pool. It is then time to realize the couple's joint life mission and to enter into joint cooperation between their energies.

In the 11th dimension, the parties are either confirmed or criticized for things they do together. This happens because the environment can sense the couple's perfect match energy. The 11th dimension is also where the first division of the couple's energy takes place, so that they can each go into the world with an individual expression that does not constantly reflect their partner's energy in the background.

In the 12th dimension, the resistance that was sent towards the couple in the 11th dimension fades. It is thus easier for them to get their respective messages through and each of the parties prepare to enter the 13th dimension at the same time.

In the 13th dimension, each party has an inner and an outer balance that attract others, as they now appear as two fully balanced Crystal Humans with all four elements of Fire, Water, Earth and Air integrated in themselves. They now have an opportunity to run completely synchronously in relation to each other with their respective energies, although they no longer spend as much time copying energies from each other, because in the 13th dimension, the parties are able to follow each other's energy from a distance.

„ANNI & THE OTHER STARS"

ABOUT ANNI SENNOV

Anni Sennov was born in 1962 and is the woman behind AuraTransformation™ which since 1996 has gained tremendous ground in Scandinavia and since 2007 has spread into the Baltic countries as well.

She works together with Berit Reaver, who is the director for The Aura Mediator Courses™, and with all other instructors on The Aura Mediator Courses™ in and outside Scandinavia.

Anni Sennov is the author of several books about AuraTransformation™, Crystal Children and Indigo Children, Relationships as well as Energy and Consciousness.

Together with her husband, Carsten Sennov, she is a partner of the publishing company Good Adventures Publishing and the coaching and consulting business SennovPartners where she consults clients on personal development, energy and consciousness.

Together, Anni and Carsten Sennov have developed the Personality Type Indicator four element profile™ that consists of four main energies corresponding to the four elements of Fire, Water, Earth and Air, which are each represented in all people in a variety of combinations of balance and strength.

Anni Sennov originally began her career in the financial world and has run her own practice, firstly with astrological counselling and healing, and then AuraTransformation™ and clairvoyance since 1993.

Anni is very direct and honest, which since 1993 has benefited her clients, the audiences who attend her presentations, as well as her readers - and she is good at giving her clients a kick in the rear, both personally and professionally.

Anni Sennov's work and books have been mentioned in numerous magazines, newspapers and on TV in Denmark, Sweden, Norway and Estonia.

You can link to Anni Sennov's profile on Facebook, Plaxo, and LinkedIn and subscribe to her newsletter at **www.annisennov.eu.**

Read more at **www.annisennov.eu**

Websites that represent Anni Sennov:

www.annisennov.eu/.dk
www.good-adventures.com/.dk
www.sennovpartners.eu/.dk
www.fourelementprofile.eu/.dk
www.auratransformation.eu/.com/co.uk/.dk/.no/.se/.fi/.co.ee/.ru/.pl/.de/
.at/.ch

Anni Sennov's authorship

Translated into other languages:

The Little Energy Guide 1 - co-author: Carsten Sennov (English)
Den lille energiguide 1 - co-author: Carsten Sennov (Danish)
Den lille energiguiden 1 - co-author: Carsten Sennov (Norwegian)
Den lilla energiguiden 1 - co-author: Carsten Sennov (Swedish)
Väike energia teejuht 1 - co-author: Carsten Sennov (Estonian)

The Crystal Human and the Crystallization Process Part I (English)
The Crystal Human and the Crystallization Process Part II (English)
Krystalmennesket & Krystalliseringsprocessen (Danish)

Crystal Children, Indigo Children & Adults of the Future (English)
Krystalbørn, Indigobørn & Fremtidens voksne (Danish)
Kristallbarn, indigobarn och framtidens vuxna (Swedish)
Kristall-lapsed, indigolapsed ja uue ajastu täiskasvanud (Estonian)
Кристальные дети,дети Индигои взрослые нового времени (Russian)

E-book:

Crystal Children, Indigo Children & Adults of the Future (English)

Current books available in Danish only:

Balance at All Levels (Balance på alle planer)
The Planet Energies Behind the Earth's Population 2005 (Planetenergierne bag Jordens befolkning 2005)

Co-author of:

The Conscious Leader (Den Bevidste Leder - currently available in Danish only) - main author: Carsten Sennov

Free e-book (currently available in Danish only):

Spirit Mates - The New Time Relationship (Åndsdualitet - Den Nye Tids parforhold) - co-author: Carsten Sennov

Sold-out titles (available in Danish only):

Karma-free in the New Time (Karma-fri i den nye tid)

Sold-out titles under the name Anni Kristoffersen (available in Danish only):

Spirit Mates - A Book About Love (Åndsdualitet - en bog om kærlighed) co-author: Carsten Sennov
The New Aura (Den nye aura)
The Planet Energies Behind the Earth's Population (Planetenergierne bag Jordens befolkning)
How Difficult Can It Be? (Hvor svært kan det være?)
The ABC of the Aura Transformation (AURA-ændringens ABC)
Masculine & Feminine Energies (Maskulin & Feminin)
Karma-free and in Harmony (Karma-fri og i harmoni!)
Daily Spiritual Energy (Åndelig energi idagligdagen)
Spiritual Energy (Åndelig energi)

Read more at **www.good-adventures.com**

Related books

The Crystal Human and the Crystallization Process Part II
by Anni Sennov

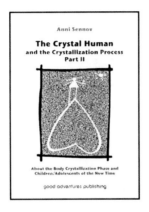

Crystal Children, Indigo Children & Adults of the Future
by Anni Sennov

See www.good-adventures.com

Related books

The Little Energy Guide 1
by Anni & Carsten Sennov

See www.good-adventures.com

Lightning Source UK Ltd.
Milton Keynes UK
UKOW031815160112

185480UK00013B/130/P